Theatre Absolute, in co-production with Warwick Arts Centre, present

ZERO

Written by Chris O'Connell
Directed by Matt Aston

Cast

Major Chaudry	Adeel Akhtar
Alex	Stephen Hudson
Demissie	Damian Lynch
Syrah	Samantha Power
Tom	Daniel Hoffmann-Gill

Creative Team

Writer	Chris O'Connell
Director	Matt Aston
Producer	Julia Negus
Original Soundscape	Andy Garbi
Design	Laura McEwen
Lighting Design	James Farncombe
Company Stage Manager	Jo James
Relights Technician	Natalie Davies
Production Manager	Sam Paterson
Design Assistant	Kate Wyatt
Dramaturg	Steve Johnstone
Artistic Associates	Paul Nolan, Lizzie Wiggs
Press	Sue Hyman Associates www.suehyman.com
Print	Pixeltrix
Production Photographs	Andrew Moore

Theatre Absolute
Institute for Creative Enterprise
Technology Park
Puma Way
Coventry
CV1 2TT
info@theateabsolute.co.uk
www.theatreabsolute.co.uk

Registered Company No: 2966897

The first performance of ZERO took place on Monday 29 September 2008 at Warwick Arts Centre, Coventry.

UK Tour Autumn 2008

Warwick Arts Centre, Coventry
29 September – 4 October

Lakeside Arts Centre, Nottingham
7 – 8 October

York Theatre Royal
10 – 11 October

Brewery Arts Centre, Kendal
14 October

The North Wall, Oxford
16 – 17 October

Contact, Manchester
21 – 22 October

Corn Exchange, Newbury
23 October

Lincoln Performing Arts Centre, Lincoln
28 – 29 October

The Brewhouse Theatre, Taunton
31 October

Lawrence Hill Church, Barton Hill, Bristol
1 November

Arena Theatre, Wolverhampton
4 November

Citizens Theatre, Glasgow
6 – 8 November

Tristan Bates Theatre, London
11 – 29 November

Theatre Absolute is a multi award winning theatre company. Founded in 1992, and based in Coventry, Theatre Absolute is a regularly funded organisation of the Arts Council, England. Its core members are Julia Negus, producer, and Chris O'Connell, artistic director and writer. The company commissions, produces and tour new plays for the theatre, which are bold, uncompromising and contemporary. Since 1999, they have earned a glowing reputation for their work, particularly through the making of *Street Trilogy* (*Car, Raw, Kid*) which thrilled audiences at the Edinburgh Festival, and toured both the UK and Europe to huge critical acclaim, and *cloud:burst*, which performed both at the Royal Opera House, London, and 59E59 Theatre, in New York City. The company places an emphasis on story and character, explored through a robust performance style and a rhythmic and heightened text, which is underpinned by soundscapes that intensify the momentum of the narrative and the experience of the audience as the world of the play gathers around them.

Plays such as *Hang Lenny Pope*, *Street Trilogy*, and *cloud:burst*, all written by Chris O'Connell, tell the story of ordinary people caught in extraordinary situations being asked huge questions that they've never faced before; they are having to survive pressure, and it's this 'do or die' reality that connects them to their humanness and their instinct to find a way to survive.

ZERO was co-commissioned by an Arts Council, England New Writing Consortium. Members of the consortium are Black Country Touring, Brewery Arts Centre, Kendal, The Brewhouse, Taunton, The Corn Exchange, Newbury, Lakeside Arts Centre, Nottingham and Theatre Royal, Bury St Edmunds. Thanks to actors Will Barton, Matt Booth, Rachel Brogan, Alex Caan, Lee Colley, John Flitcroft, Clive Llewellyn, and Connie M'Gadzah for their work on developing ZERO and to Nick Giles, Director at The Corn Exchange, Newbury, for hosting a Writing House script week in October 2007.

Learning and access is an integral part of Theatre Absolute's core activities. During the creation and production of ZERO, the company appointed Joe Hammond as writer-in-residence, and as part of The Works, the company's in-house independent theatre apprenticeship scheme, students from Cardinal Newman school participated in a series of workshops which tracked the creation of the project from script development, to premiere. For more details of The Works and other participatory activities please contact the company.

Absolute thanks to the following people for their support on ZERO:

Nell Bailey, Chris Billings, Brian Bishop, Neil Darlison, Rachel Brogan, Georgina Egan, John Flitcroft, Alison Gagen, John Ginman, Christine Hamilton, Graeme Hawley, Kellie Keith, Steve Johnstone, Carolyn Jolliffe, Jacinta Nordone, Claire Maddocks, Sooki McShane, Andrew Moore, Julie Moore, Sandra Moore, Paul Nolan, Ben O'Brien, Joanna Reid, Andrew Riley, Martin Sutherland, Rachel Sutton, Lizzie Wiggs.

Thanks to all at Warwick Arts Centre, the New Writing Consortium and Arts Council England for supporting ZERO.

Winners Edinburgh Fringe First 2001
Winners Edinburgh Fringe First 1999
Winners Time Out Live Award (London) 1999

AN INTRODUCTION TO THE PLAY ZERO

ZERO continues the dominant themes of Theatre Absolute's previous work, placing ordinary people in extraordinary situations. It is a play made up of twin obsessions: the pulverising grip of capitalism and its effect on the individual; and the onset of conscience, a time when a person is gripped and disturbed and unsettled by events around them, a time when one's inner voice won't be stilled, insisting that *you* as a citizen of the world should care, should *act*.

I am still chilled by memories of the TV footage from 1989 showing tanks moving across Tiananmen Square, and the brave unknown rebel who stood in front of the tanks and refused to move. In ZERO, the character of Alex is in some way constructed from visions of that lone soul in that empty space, doing his stuff against forces much stronger, and more deadly. To me that man is a defining vision of resistance - the insistence that the territory of one's mind and soul will not be tampered with. Of course, resistance dies if the baton isn't handed on, which is where Alex's journey begins and ends.

There is also the element of torture. Are those who are responsible for torture in ZERO, also acting from conscience? Information is needed, obsessions grow, and whatever means are necessary can be justified. But the character Syrah isn't a thug, she doesn't look like a monster, she is educated, and believes that morally she is sworn to act for the sake of her unborn child. It's a compelling standpoint. Conscience can cut both ways. It's a reminder that to ask a bloodthirsty world to listen to its conscience won't necessarily save it from further brutalities.

And if conscience isn't hard enough, where is it all heading? This 'money' thing. This system that has outlived communism, socialism and all the other 'isms'.

ZERO takes place in a camp where 'terrorists' are interrogated and tortured in order to gain information about who finances and who arms them. But I was keen that ZERO isn't seen as a Guantanamo Bay play, or a play about Iraq, or Afghanistan. These will be clear references for any audience member, but the play is set twenty years in the future and the stakes for the characters are different; they are pitched beyond struggles as currently tangible to us as religious ideology, or regime change.

In ZERO, the audience are thrown into a nightmare world in which the relentless pursuit of profit, and the politics of envy sit centre stage. I wanted to write a play that imagines the next crisis that we as a human race will stumble into, (although it feels like it's already there, rubbing its hands in anticipation). Yet we choose to ignore it. No one wants to debate the downside of capitalism because there are so many benefits, yet it is slowly ripping the heart out of us, and reducing us to savages.

If people are angry now in 2008 as British Petroleum make 16 billion dollars annual profit, if we are angry at soaring food prices, if we feel stretched now by taxes and the price of utilities, ZERO asks the audience to imagine a world 20, 30 years from now when the world's assets have been stripped beyond recognition, and the pockets of the rich lined ever deeper. How will people feel, and how will they act?

ZERO is clearly heightened. All of my plays live in 'what if worlds'; they are dark and blatantly intense. But I think they always feel real. The future may prove ZERO to be inaccurate or unfounded, but as a play ZERO is a guttural airing of modern day fears, shared not only by myself as a writer, but by every day ordinary people, the wisest most unaffected sort, who can often sense something in the air long before it arrives.

Chris O'Connell
August 2008

CAST AND CREATIVE TEAM

Chris O'Connell
Writer

Chris was writer-in-residence for Paines Plough, 1999-2000, and most recently was Playwright in Residence at Birmingham University, attached to their M(Phil) in playwriting, 2005-2006. Plays for Theatre Absolute include: *Hang Lenny Pope* (National Tour 2007), *cloud:burst* (Royal Opera House, London 2005/ 59E59 Theatre, New York 2006), and *Car, Raw* and *Kid* (Edinburgh Festival, national and European tours, 1999-2003). *Car* and *Raw* won Fringe First Awards for Outstanding New Work and Innovation at the Edinburgh Fringe Festivals 1999 and 2001 respectively. *Car* won a Time Out Live Award for Best New Play on the London Fringe, 1999 and the three plays were performed as *Street Trilogy* and toured throughout the UK in Spring 2005. Other work includes: *The Crossing Bridge* (EGO Performance Company), *Tall Phoenix* (Belgrade Theatre), *Thyestes* (RSC), *Hymns* (Frantic Assembly), *Hold Ya'* (Red Ladder Theatre Co), *Auto* (Vanemuine Theatre, Estonia), *Cool Water Murder* (Belgrade Theatre), *The Blue Zone* (mac Productions), *Gabriel's Ashes* (BBC Radio 4) and *Eastenders* (BBC1). His work has been both read and produced in Estonia, Italy, Australia and America.

Matt Aston
Director

Matt has been Programmer and Producer at the Djanogly Theatre, Lakeside Arts Centre, Nottingham, since the venue first opened in 2001. Previously as Producer at Nottingham Playhouse he was responsible for programming visiting events and managing projects including Jamaica House (East Midlands Tour); Community productions of *Robin Hood – A Musical Celebration*, *Cold Comfort Farm*; and *Samuel Beckett's First Love* which included a short European Tour. He directed two plays in the Playhouse's Volcanic Season: *Heaven of David's* by Tim Wood; and *Velvet Afternoon with Dave Velour*, which he also wrote. Matt was also Assistant Director on Nottingham Playhouse's Community production of *Macbeth*. In spring 2003, Matt directed Kenneth Alan Taylor in Lakeside's first in-house production – *Krapp's Last Tape* by Samuel Beckett. In December 2003 he re-directed Macrobert Arts Centre's *The Happy Prince*. Matt subsequently went on to direct Lakeside in-house productions – *A Different Way Home* by Jimmie Chinn, *A Visit from Miss Prothero* by Alan Bennett, *A Who's Who of Flapland* by David Halliwell, *The Retirement of Tom Stevens* by William Ivory (Premiere), *The Kiss* by Glyn Cannon (Premiere) and *Smile* by Stephen Lowe (Premiere) and co-directed *Twinkle Little Star* by Philip Meeks. In 2005 Matt directed *Samuel's Head On My Table* by Declan Keen for the Momentum Young Writer's Festival and has directed the rehearsed readings of

Silence by Ivar Waldemarson as part of the 2006 festival and *Smile* by Stephen Lowe as part of the 2007 festival. Matt represents Lakeside Arts Centre on the Arts Council England New Writing Consortium who originally commissioned ZERO. He has been involved in the development of the play from the outset and is delighted to be working with Chris O'Connell and Theatre Absolute to see ZERO through to its premiere production and tour.

Julia Negus
Producer

Trained at Webber Douglas Academy of Dramatic Art, London, Julia co-founded Theatre Absolute in 1992 with writer Chris O'Connell. She has produced all of the company's work to date, including *Car* (Edinburgh Fringe First 99, Time Out Award 99, national and international tours 2000), *Raw* (Edinburgh Fringe First 01 and national tour 2002), *Kid* (Edinburgh Festival 2003), *Street Trilogy*, (national tour 2005), *cloud: burst* (Firsts Festival, Royal Opera House 2005, Brits Off Broadway, New York City 2005), *Hang Lenny Pope* (national tour 2007).

Andy Garbi
Soundscape

Described in the May '08 issue of Classic FM magazine as "the ambassador of British new music" and current featured artist on BBC Radio 3's Late Junction, Andy Garbi's cutting edge vocal and composition work have gained the support of leading artists in all fields of the performing arts. He has worked with artists such as Nigel Kennedy and appeared on the same bill as The Prodigy, Roni Size, Transglobal Underground, Square Pusher, Jah Wobble and Massive Attack. Andy has also headlined major stages at Glastonbury, The Big Chill, The Big Green Gathering, Windows on The World, Ely Folk Festival and the biggest world music festival in France the Trans Musicale. In the last 4 years alone has worked with Birmingham Royal Ballet, been selected twice to represent the UK internationally for music, gained a distinction for his masters degree in composition, created numerous scores for award-winning plays and has himself received: The Channel 4 Film Music Award, The PRS Foundation Award for Advances Toward Original Music, The Birmingham Conservatoire Masters Prize. As well as writing and performing his own music, Andy also works with theatre, film, ballet and contemporary dance. His debut solo album 'The Sound of One' is currently receiving critical acclaim from a hugely diverse range of the national and international press.

James Farncombe
Lighting Design

James is a freelance lighting designer, based in London. Previous productions for Theatre Absolute include *cloud:burst*, *Street Trilogy* and *Hang Lenny Pope*. Recent work includes: *2000 Feet Away* and *Tinderbox*, Bush Theatre, *Breaking the Silence*, Nottingham Playhouse; *Turandot* and *Taking*

Care of Baby, Hampstead Theatre; The *Glass Menagerie* New Wolsey, Ipswich. This year, he was nominated for a Clay Pakey Knights of Illumination award for The Dysfunckshunals at the Bush, and was shortlisted for the 2008 Arts Foundation Fellowship for Lighting Design. He is an artistic associate of the Bush Theatre.

Laura McEwen
Design

Laura trained at Nottingham Trent University. She has designed numerous shows for Nottingham Playhouse, most recently *Tom's Midnight Garden* and *The Dumb Waiter*. Other companies she has worked for include; Pilot Theatre Company, York Theatre Royal, Polka Theatre, Southwark Playhouse, Sheffield Crucible, Red Earth Theatre, Unicorn Theatre and the English National Opera Bayliss Programme. Recent work includes *We're going on a Bear Hunt* Polka Theatre, London, *The Crane* Red Earth Theatre and *Smile*, Lakeside Art Centre. She enjoys designing for a range of spaces and this has included studios, main stages, parks, community centres, school halls, classrooms and site-specific environments. In 2005 Laura won the Manchester Evening News Design Award for *Beautiful Thing* at the Bolton Octagon. As well as designing, she frequently works as a creative workshop leader, employed by Theatre in Education companies, youth theatres, galleries, schools and community groups. Laura has a specific interest in new and devised work and is associate director of Red Earth Theatre Company.

Jo James
Company Stage Manager

Jo is a freelance stage manager who trained at Rose Bruford and is based in Nottingham. Theatres and touring companies she has worked for include: Oily Cart, Roundabout TIE, Quicksilver, Theatre Alibi, Leicester Haymarket, Nottingham Playhouse, Lakeside Arts Centre and York Theatre Royal.

Adeel Akhtar
Major Chaudry

Adeel Akhtar trained at the Actors Studio Drama School in New York, where his wide-ranging roles included, Biff in *Death of a Salesman* and Lloyd in *Mud*. Since his graduation, Adeel has appeared in numerous television dramas, such as *Law and Order* and *Conviction* in the US and *Britz* and Linda La Plante's *Trial and Retribution* in the UK. Adeel has also starred in a number of short films, including *The Pope's Face*, which won the Audience Choice Award at the Millbrook International 3-Minute Film Festival. He recently returned from Marseilles where he worked opposite Guy Pearce in the up-coming feature film *Traitor*. Adeel's most notable theatre role was as Khaled in *Back of the Throat* at New York's Flea Theatre, for which he received praise both in Time Out and in the New York Times. Adeel is part of an action theatre improvisation group, and helps organise a monthly performance night, bringing together London artists from diverse backgrounds.

Stephen Hudson
Alex

Trained at the Drama Centre London. Theatre includes *The Revenger's Tragedy, An Ideal Husband* (Manchester Royal Exchange), *Cyrano de Bergerac* (Bristol Old Vic), *The Kiss* (Nottingham Lakeside), *After Miss Julie* (Nottingham Playhouse), *Journey's End* (Duke of Yorks & Tour), *Lady Windemere's Fan* (Theatre Royal Haymarket), *Two Sisters and a Piano* (Riverside), *Mincemeat* (Cardboard Citizens), *Peer Gynt* (BAC), *Lady Windemere's Fan* (Windsor & Tour), *Rosencrantz and Guildenstern Are Dead* (Arcola), *Kristendom* (Bridewell), *Treatment* and *Wolfboy* (Finborough Theatre), *The Seagull* (Perserverance Theatre, Alaska). TV includes *Holby City, Doctors, Spooks, EastEnders, The Bill.* Film includes *A Good Year, Eye Candy, Sweet Thing, Resolution.*

Demissie
Damian Lynch

Training at the Webber Douglas Academy in London. Theatre credits include: *A Brief Summary* (Paines Plough/Shakespeare's Globe), *200 Years* (Watford Palace Theatre), *23 Greatest Moments of Dave, The Miniaturists* (Arcola Theatre), *Carthage Must Be Destroyed* (Traverse, Edinburgh – Winner of Best New Play at CATS award 2007-8), and *School for Scandal* (Salisbury Playhouse). Television and film credits include; *GSG9* (Typhoon AG Germany), *The Bill, Little Britain,*

Waking the Dead, Judge John Deed and *Munich.* Recent productions for radio include: *A Long Way from Home* (Radio 3), *Small Island, The Resistible Rise of Arturo Ui* and *Metropolis* (all for Radio 4 and World Service Drama). Damian was winner of the BBC Carleton Hobbs Radio Award 2003 and twice a member of the BBC Radio Drama Company. He recently narrated the autobiography of Johnson Beharry VC, *Barefoot Soldier: A Tale of Extreme Valour.*

Samantha Power
Syrah

Samantha trained at the Welsh College of Music and Drama. Her television credits include: *Shameless, Massive, The Cup* (Series Regular), *Doctors, It's Adam and Shelley, Little Britain Abroad, New Street Law, Little Britain* Series 2 and 3, *Twisted Tales, The Royal, Barbara, Where the Heart Is, The Safe House, The Cops, City Central, Peak Practice, A Prince Among Men* (two series), *Spoofovision – Mash and Peas, Coronation Street, No Bananas.* For Theatre: Flint Street Nativity, Liverpool Playhouse. Australian Tour *Little Britain Live,* UK Tour *Little Britain Live. Iron,* Contact Theatre. *Coming Around Again* and *Accrington Pals* for West Yorkshire Playhouse, *Little Malcolm,* Bolton Octagon, *Educating Rita,* Brighton Hove Theatre Company, *The Importance of Being Earnest* and *Spring and Port Wine,* National Tours. *School Daze,* Riverside Studios. *The Sound Collector,* M6 Theatre Company.

For Theatre Absolute: *Street Trilogy*, *Kid* and *Raw* (Awarded a Fringe First 2001).
Her Film Credits include: *Mischief Night* and *The Low Down*.
Radio: *Little Britain The Complete Series*.

Daniel Hoffmann-Gill
Tom

Daniel trained at the Central School of Speech and Drama and is a founder member of Blurred Clarity for whom he has written, directed and performed: *Carnival, Hobchob's Choice, The Home, [fragments : BODIES], LINK, Free From Fear* and *Human Shrapnel*, all of which toured nationally. Other theatre includes *The Lesson* (White Bear Theatre), *BED* (BAC), *Dreams Come Out To Play* (Birmingham Rep), a large scale tour of *Bouncers* with Reform Theatre, *Passenger Action* (Embassy Theatre), *Coast to Coast, The Big Adventure, Thick as Thieves* and *Bedders and Pike* (all Hard Graft/National Tour) and two site-specific pieces: *You Are Here* and *Fade to Black*. Daniel has just finished shooting his first feature film, *My Last Five Girlfriends*, directed by BAFTA winner Julian Kemp, starring opposite Naomie Harris and Brendan Patricks. Television includes: *Behind The Banner* (Channel 4), *The Fastest Milk Float In The World* (Carlton), *Emmerdale, Heartbeat* (both Yorkshire), *Peak Practice* (Carlton), *Dangerfield* (BBC) and numerous commercials across the world.
Daniel's blog is at:
http://danielhg.blogspot.com

warwick arts centre

Warwick Arts Centre is driven by the imagination and creativity of today's artists and maintains an enviable position of being one of the most adventurous and innovative arts spaces in the UK. Our aim is to place contemporary arts and culture firmly within the everyday lives of the region's audiences. We do this by commissioning, producing and presenting those artists we believe to be the most exciting and innovative and those that we think will have something to say to our audiences. We hope that our response to the changing theatrical landscape of the UK has become ever more distinctive and with five performing spaces (soon to be six), our commitment to our theatre programme is threefold: to support theatre companies, writers, actors, directors and producers living and working in the locality; to support and explore the creation of new forms of theatre by companies and theatre makers across the UK; to present a programme of the most exciting international theatre available.

Warwick Arts Centre has maintained a long association with Theatre Absolute. In 2005 we embarked upon a major collaboration to produce and tour the award winning trilogy of plays written by Chris O'Connell, *Car*, *Raw* and *Kid* under the banner *Street Trilogy*. At the same time we commissioned a new play by Chris O'Connell, *cloud:burst*. *Hang Lenny Pope* was our third collaborative adventure and we are delighted to be co-producing *Zero* for the autumn of 2008.

Alan Rivett   Neil Darlison

Warwick Arts Centre
September 2008

ZERO

To the memory of Sheila O'Connell

First published in 2008 by Oberon Books Ltd
521 Caledonian Road, London N7 9RH
Tel: 020 7607 3637 / Fax: 020 7607 3629
e-mail: info@oberonbooks.com
www.oberonbooks.com

A catalogue record for this book is available from the British Library.

ISBN: 978-1-84002-881-2

Cover design by Pixeltrix

Cast

MAJOR CHAUDRY

ALEX

DEMISSIE MULENEH

TOM

SYRAH

SOLDIERS

SOLDIER 1 **doubles with** SYRAH;
SOLDIER 2 **with** DEMISSIE

The action takes place in a not too distant future, some of it in Camp Zero, some of it in a room. The room may be in a very run down hotel, or maybe a disused shack. It's somewhere indistinct and desperate. A cupboard, a window. Perhaps two beds, perhaps just two mattresses on the floor.

Note: The symbol / donates an interruption point.

ONE

The sound of a helicopter.

SYRAH, ALEX, and the MAJOR watch as DEMISSIE
MULENEH strolls across the space and writes ten
words on a wall. The MAJOR reads the words, as
DEMISSIE writes.

MAJOR: i committed suicide because of the brutality of my
crimes.

ALEX: no he didn't.

MAJOR: what?

ALEX: he didn't.

MAJOR: that's what he's written.

ALEX: don't believe what you're seeing.

MAJOR: why would he write it?

ALEX: he didn't.

MAJOR: (To DEMISSIE MULENEH.) is it true that you killed /
yourself because of…?

DEMISSIE: why does it matter?

MAJOR: what?

DEMISSIE: i said why does it matter?

MAJOR: because you wrote it.

ALEX: i need to call my wife…

DEMISSIE: (To MAJOR.) come and help me.

MAJOR: yes sir.

DEMISSIE: (Of TOM.) grab him.

MAJOR: yes sir.

TOM is dragged in by DEMISSIE, and the MAJOR.
Trussed up in chains and blindfolded, TOM is unable
to move.

DEMISSIE: Initial Reaction Force: pose one.

MAJOR: sir!

> They stop and twist TOM round, posing him grotesquely for a camera that DEMISSIE holds. He takes a photo of TOM.

DEMISSIE: Initial Reaction Force: pose two.

MAJOR: sir!

DEMISSIE: burn it. archive it.

MAJOR: sir!

DEMISSIE: make sure i get a copy.

MAJOR: sir!

ALEX: i'm going to call my wife. zero, zero…

DEMISSIE: (Hurling ALEX's phone into the darkness.) no.

ALEX: hey!!!

DEMISSIE: up.

ALEX: bastard!

> TOM is hoisted into the air, upside down.

MAJOR: if a man commits suicide because of the brutality of his crimes, then there must be a hundred more with the same story, is that right sir?

ALEX: (Of the mobile.) what did you do with it?

DEMISSIE: if there *are* stories…

ALEX: (Of the mobile.) give it back.

MAJOR: must be hundreds, is that right sir?

DEMISSIE: we don't mention it.

ALEX: (Of the mobile.) give me the phone back.

MAJOR: what sort of stories?

DEMISSIE: hit him.

MAJOR: do we believe in them?

DEMISSIE: we don't mention it.

ALEX: my wife's going to save me.

DEMISSIE: hit him.

ALEX: the tone of her voice.

MAJOR: (Hitting TOM.) you are not subject to the laws of the geneva convention, or any of the conditions attached thereof.

ALEX: the voice of an angel. i need to speak to her, and taking his mobile isn't going to stop me.

MAJOR: (To TOM.) you are a prisoner not of conscience, but of violence. you have bombed, and maimed. you are subject to the rules of torture under the agreement of the global economic alliance. you are here because you have broken the rules laid out for you on your arrival at the camp. you will be broken. your only hope will be to sip from a single box of rain left at the door of your cage, to quench your thirst, in the barren endlessness of your capture, here, at the camp.

ALEX: *stop it.*

DEMISSIE: a box of fucking rain.

MAJOR: the camp.

DEMISSIE: *if* that.

ALEX: she's called fiona.

SYRAH: he'll be unconscious in ten seconds.

TOM: alex.

> MAJOR hits TOM. Although she counts, SYRAH leaves all the hitting of ALEX to the MAJOR.

SYRAH: one.

TOM: *alex!!*

SYRAH: two.

MAJOR: i want to hit him again.

ALEX: fiona.

MAJOR: three. there must be hundreds who commit suicide because of the brutality of their crimes.

SYRAH: four.

ALEX: there are.

MAJOR / SYRAH: five.

ALEX: this guy didn't kill himself anyway.

SYRAH: six.

MAJOR: i don't understand.

TOM: no one said this would happen!

DEMISSIE: hit him.

MAJOR / SYRAH: seven.

TOM: you said i was taking part in an exercise.

MAJOR: the fucker needs breaking. (With SYRAH.) eight.

ALEX: it wasn't suicide, none of it's suicide, *i've been in the camp, it's all there in the / book, the fucking…*

DEMISSIE: hit him.

ALEX: jesus…

MAJOR / SYRAH: nine.

TOM: *alex!!*

MAJOR hits TOM, who screams.

ALEX: *stop it. (*He grabs DEMISSIE.*) demissie.*

TOM: *i shouldn't be here!!*

DEMISSIE: (To ALEX.) who?

SYRAH: ten.

ALEX: demissie. it's me, it's alex, make it stop, i'm trying to ring my wife.

DEMISSIE: who is demissie?

MAJOR hits TOM, he screams.

ALEX: you are…and / i'm…i'm…

MAJOR: (Looking off.) the presidents have just arrived.

ALEX: …zero, zero, nine, four / *i can't remember the number, what's the fucking number…?*

MAJOR, now joined by DEMISSIE, beats TOM.

MAJOR / DEMISSIE: you are not subject to the laws of the geneva convention, or any of the conditions attached thereof. you are a prisoner not of conscience, but of violence. you have bombed, and maimed.

DEMISSIE: he's spinning nicely.

ALEX: stop it.

MAJOR: (Looking off.) the presidents are watching.

The two men beat TOM, he screams in pain.

ALEX: get him down.

DEMISSIE: *impress.*

ALEX: *I SAID GET HIM DOWN WE'RE ON THE SAME FUCKING SIDE!!!*

DEMISSIE: *impress.*

SYRAH: you don't know the story.

ALEX: i've been with him fifteen weeks for christ's sake, we arrived on the same day, *fifteen weeks at the same fucking camp so don't tell me I DON'T KNOW THE STORY!!!!!*

TOM: what story?

They lower TOM down.

ALEX: you're distracting me, i *know* the story, get-him-down-so-i-can-ring-my-wife…

TOM: *what fucking story?!!!!!!*

ALEX: i know how *all* of the stories are *all* connected, his, mine, yours, *fuck,* you're distracting me *SO MUCH* my head hurts and i want to call my wife, you're distracting me, and the story is, the *story* is why i'm here…

TOM: (Calmly.) what story?

ALEX: the story is why i want to call my wife. please. just. the story is...

He lies back onto his bed, stares at the ceiling. He sighs, almost sleeping.

don't tell me i don't know the story.

The helicopter sound stops.

TWO

A room. A hideout in the bush. Two beds. An A4 sized heavily bound package.

TOM: What story?

ALEX sits up on the bed.

You sleeping?

No answer.

Got any coffee stashed away anywhere?

ALEX: Where did you go?

TOM: Talking to yourself.

No answer

What story?

ALEX: Did you see anyone?

TOM: No one knows we're here isn't it.

ALEX: Not yet they don't.

TOM: There's no one around. I went out to find coffee, cos you're just sleeping isn't it? I need coffee and I need cigs, and you're away with the fairies.

ALEX crosses to the package.

ALEX: What's this doing here?

TOM: Did you ring her?

ALEX: Tom.

TOM: You were sleeping.

ALEX: Why's it over here?

TOM: What?

ALEX: Did you open it?

TOM: You put it there yourself. / So you didn't ring her?

ALEX: Tom.

TOM: *No, I didn't.*

> ALEX lies down again on the bed. He puts the package under the pillow.

ALEX: I don't understand why it was over there.

> TOM waits.

> (Of the package.) So you didn't open it?

TOM: *Jesus, fucking parrot in my ear isn't it?* No. Not that I can see what the problem is, you know what I'm saying? Not like I'm going to review the fucker isn't it? / Not like I'm going to...

ALEX: *Alright.*

TOM: You're the one brought it up.

ALEX: So let's drop it.

TOM: Stole my fucking words man.

ALEX: You wanted the money.

TOM: Let me read it.

ALEX: How many / times've we...

TOM: I'll read it now. I'll go for a shit and / I'll read it on the...

ALEX: *No.*

> ALEX stops. Silence. TOM stares at him.

TOM: State of you man.

> Silence.

How long we been here?

Silence.

I want coffee.

Silence.

What we doing then?

ALEX: Lying down. Lie back down.

TOM: How's lying down going to help us? We're lost, we're hungry. We could give it all up.

ALEX: Yeah.

TOM: Just like that.

ALEX: Yeah.

TOM: So all this shit about / ringing your wife…

ALEX: It's not shit. We're best friends. Before I do anything, / I always…

TOM: Not about writing your book though isn't it? Wouldn't be in this room now. *Cooped.* Can't stand being cooped, not a day longer isn't it? We're on the run, we're *cooped* and you want to ring your fucking wife.

ALEX: Because / I said…

TOM: You *said.* Yeah. / What *did* you say?

ALEX: I said I'd ring her and ask her if she / thinks we're doing the…

TOM: Which we're not, you fucking *mong.*

ALEX: In your opinion. / But I… *Remember who you're talking to!!!*

TOM: Yeah? Or what? *You.* I'm talking to *you.* (He starts again. Calmer.) And *I've* said, like a million times, this ain't going to work out in our favour. *Sir.* Don't matter how we look at it, don't matter where we hide, there's brass out there wanna teach us a lesson, top fucking brass pissed off with you and your book bad mouthing them isn't it?

ALEX shoots a look at TOM. TOM feels his stare. He raises his eyebrows: 'what?'

ALEX: No one knows about the book.

TOM: What?

ALEX: No one / *knows* about the...

TOM: Yeah.

ALEX: So what are you saying?

TOM: I'm not saying anything. Alex, fuck's sake, *I'm delirious,* I'm standing by that window and I can see the world isn't it?

ALEX: We're in the bush.

TOM: *I want to get back to it all.*

He stops. Silence.

Isn't it? I could kill someone I feel so bad.

ALEX turns onto his side, away from TOM, clutching the pillow and the package. TOM cracks.

RIGHT!!!! RIGHT! FUCKING... SO YOU DON'T WANT TO LISTEN TO ME, YOU DON'T GIVE A FUCK... FUCK'S SAKE. THAT'S IT, IF YOU WON'T FUCKING, IF YOU WON'T FUCKING... ISN'T IT. ISN'T IT!!! IF YOU WON'T RING YOUR WIFE, IF YOU WON'T LISTEN TO WHAT I WANT, THEN YOU NEED TO LET ME SEE WHAT YOU WROTE... AT LEAST! ISN'T IT? I GOT A RIGHT TO KNOW HOW SMELLY THIS SHIT IS... THIS SHIT YOU'VE GOT US IN ALEX... THIS FUCKING... I'VE GOT A RIGHT TO...TO...TO...

He stops. He lies back on the bed. Long long silence.

ALEX: What was there?

TOM looks over at ALEX.

How did we get here?

TOM continues to look at ALEX.

TOM: Fuck's sake. I don't know… Everything was just… Isn't it?

ALEX: Was it?

THREE

Three months earlier.

The sound of jeeps, engines idling, and helicopters arriving and leaving. TOM and ALEX with army issue back packs.

ALEX: We'll be moving soon.

TOM: It's all the jeeps. They're backed right up.

Pause.

How big is this place?

ALEX: Lieutenant Brines, by the way.

TOM: Yeah? Right. What are you here for then, / are you a cook, or…?

ALEX: Translator.

TOM: Nice one. (Indicates himself.) Squaddie. Guard. Something like that, fuck's sake, I don't know. Tom.

TOM offers to shake hands, realises it's inappropriate and salutes ALEX instead.

Sir.

ALEX: (Wry.) If you make that Sir sound any more sarcastic, I'll have to discipline you.

TOM looks at him.

Joke.

TOM: Only joined five months ago. Want to go back in time isn't it?

ALEX: You'll soon get the feel for it.

TOM: Five months ago I'm in the recruitment office down the town; answering the call up, isn't it? Five months ago I'm scrawling on the dotted line. Didn't think I'd end up here.

ALEX: *What did you think?*

TOM: *Said they need good men.*

ALEX: *You look pretty good to me.*

TOM: *Didn't seem too bothered who I was to be honest. Get that signature, boom, bang, off you go. It's hot man. I'm fucked and I'm five months in.*

ALEX: *I've learnt. I'm a Lieutenant.*

TOM: *Sir?*

ALEX: *I can give you some advice. It'll either help you, or you can ignore it.*

TOM watches him.

I've been here six months.

TOM: *So what you doing stood here with me?*

ALEX: *I was on Side One. (He points.) Over the estuary; admin, PR. The camp's got two sides.*

TOM: (Does a DJ 'scratching' impression.) *Like the vinyl yeah? You ain't been in Side Two yet then?*

ALEX: *Only a short induction, last week. But I'm saying, I've done tours in North Korea, Iran. Keep it easy. Don't stress about anything you can't change. Stay on message, do what's asked of you; get home.*

TOM: *You seen any of them?*

ALEX: *Who?*

TOM: *The scum.*

ALEX shakes his head.

Can't wait isn't it? That's why I signed up. (Shunts his elbow.) Duff. Dirty men, bombing my people.

ALEX: *Bombing / your…?*

TOM: *Yeah. You saying they're not dirty? Sergeant says to me on the chopper, 'get your stamping boots ready'.*

ALEX: *Is that what he said?*

TOM: *Bloke at the recruiting office says it's about collective enemies.*

ALEX: *I don't like to talk in those terms.*

TOM: *See me, I've lost ten people in two years. Ten man!*

ALEX: *Sir.*

TOM: *Sir. Yeah. Five killed when they blasted the tunnel, three dead on ferries. Not all family, but it's friends, you lose people. How long we got to live like this isn't it? The idea of revenge…*

ALEX: *Is that what it is?*

TOM: *That's what they said I could get when I was in the recruiting office.*

ALEX: *Revenge for what?*

TOM: *We've lost our way of life isn't it?*

ALEX: *Have we?*

TOM: *You get on a plane and there's some dodgy bastard at the back, he's not talking, but he's got that look. The scum's got that look ain't they?*

ALEX: *You mean The Others.*

TOM: *The Others, The Outsiders, whatever we're told to call them; s'all politics talk isn't it? Scum basically. But yeah, this guy, he's one of The Other's then, you saying you won't get the pilot to check him out? Double check him, triple check him isn't it? Better still, don't let him fly with the rest of us. The 'rest of us', fucking laugh that is though isn't it? Who's talking to who? No fucker isn't it? Sir. Summer, that's changed as well. No more enjoying the sun, fucking curfews and smoke screens everywhere isn't it.*

ALEX: *It doesn't feel real.*

TOM: *Disaster movie isn't it.*

ALEX: *That we've got to this point.*

TOM: *Well this is real.*

    ALEX *looks at him.*

    Camp Zero. If we ever get there. (Smiles.) Isn't it?

They wait. Then…

ALEX: *We're moving.*

TOM: **Cool.**

They walk forward. Blackout.

FOUR

The camp. The sound of a helicopter.

DEMISSIE MULENEH, a prisoner at Camp Zero, lies in a pool of light, caged. ALEX and TOM hit the space, their back packs with them. Before them is an x-ray system.

A voice is heard on a tannoy.

VOICE: **In.**

TOM walks forward.

VOICE: **Wait for the x-ray. Don't move.**

Light swells on TOM. He waits.

VOICE: **What's that in your pocket?**

TOM: **What?**

VOICE: **What's that in your pocket? Bottom right.**

TOM looks to his trouser pocket.

TOM: **Nothing, I emptied everything, I…**

VOICE: **There's something in your pocket.**

TOM forages inside, brings out a tiny straggly bit of tissue.

VOICE: **Identify it.**

TOM: **Tissue. I've been a bit…**

He indicates a snuffly nose.

Long long silence. Then…

VOICE: **Next.**

TOM passes through. ALEX follows. He waits as the x-ray circles him. He is clear.

In.

Out.

TOM and ALEX unshoulder their packs. The voice continues.

Welcome to Camp Zero. You have arrived in Side Two. In Side Two, security means survival. There is no other way in, and no other way out. No breaches of security will be tolerated. As decreed by the presidents, all information is controlled, how it is revealed and the rate at which any revelations are sanctioned, ie information on detainees, numbers of detainees, states of mind of detainees, methods of interrogation used on detainees, personal successes and failures of various said detainees, is all controlled. Do not be tempted to counteract this.

As the voice continues, TOM carries a box towards DEMISSIE; he passes ALEX who is heading the other way. ALEX watches TOM as he lays the box of rain down by the door of DEMISSIE's cage. DEMISSIE rolls onto his back and looks at TOM. They stare at each other.

Other matters: on Side Two we enjoy the company of many geckos. They are considered to be natural, beautiful, and a protected species. Whilst we are here on what is, effectively, their land, we must respect their rights. Any soldier abusing the rights of geckos, or driving over them, will be subject to a 15,000 note fine.

Straight ahead is the compound. To the right, are the cages. There are 4000 units, each one contains a detainee.The cages are your territory. Guard them. Mess over there, computers, jacuzzi, pool, gym, running track, DVD and video messaging, X-Box, PS12, Wii and intranet, all over there. Officers quarters, there. Privates, quick march.

Blackout.

FIVE

The camp. Night. At the edge of the compound. ALEX approaches.

ALEX: No stars.

TOM: (Jumps.) Fuck.

ALEX: Sorry.

Pause.

You alright?

TOM: Yeah. You? Settled in alright?

ALEX: You're looking glum.

TOM: Homesick.

ALEX: Already.

TOM: Two days isn't it?

ALEX: Remember what I said.

TOM: You said I should keep it easy. Got a spare ciggie?

ALEX: No cigarettes after ten.

TOM: Fuck that isn't it? I need one man.

ALEX: Sir.

TOM: Sir. Sorry. Did you see any of them yet? I'm shaking.

ALEX: Keep it easy.

TOM slaps a hand on his face.

TOM: My cheek, see it twitching. My hands, my legs, all up my thighs. Twitching, since supper. Since I saw them. Just the one. I saw him. Just one. He was in his cage. Swing a fucking ant in there, yeah? No chance isn't it? Sarge says to me, 'You're ready for your first detail. Take these boxes to the cage compound.' Face to face. Seeing one of those murderers, I was... I stared at him. Is this one of them? After all the stories, are these really the people? Isn't it? Can't believe that. Here. In the camp. My head's the worst...

ALEX: See a medic.

TOM: *I'm spinning…*

TOM turns and throws up.

Fuck!! FUCK!! *(Shouts at the camp, into the darkness.)* **Look how you've made me feel…!!!**

ALEX: *Control yourself.*

TOM: *Sir.*

Silence. ALEX waits.

Let me go home… This is wrong… I… What's your name…?

ALEX: *Lieutenant Brines.*

TOM: *I mean your first name, fucking bowing and scraping around man, it's not what I do…*

ALEX: *It's how it's done here.*

TOM: *So fuck it. I don't want to do it like this… I want… I… We could meet, every night. Here. We could meet for a chat isn't it? Tell each other about our lives, our birds. You got a bird? I'll come down, I'll meet you here.*

TOM chucks up again, thrown off balance by the force of his vomiting, groaning, like a man dying. ALEX waits, holds him by the arm.

You're kind.

ALEX: *I'm excusing your behaviour. You're still adjusting.*

TOM breathes, calms.

TOM: *I owe you one.*

SIX

The hideout. ALEX dials on a mobile. Stops, can't think of the next number. He hits his forehead with the heel of his hand, once, twice.

TOM: (Calmly.) **Alex.** *Alex.*

ALEX stops.

Calm it, isn't it?

Pause.

ALEX: Where's the book?

TOM looks to the package ALEX is clutching to his side.

(Of the package.) You're not trashing this by the way.

TOM: What?

ALEX: Before you get any ideas.

TOM: I wasn't.

ALEX: We're not giving in.

TOM: (Weary.) Just ring her isn't it? You said it yourself, you'll ring your wife, see what / she's got to……

ALEX: I said I'd *ask* her.

TOM: Yeah, cos that's fair, there being two of us, and me being in the shit as well isn't it?

ALEX: Yeah.

TOM: Cool. So try again. Breathe.

ALEX focuses on the mobile.

ALEX: (He breathes. Dials.) Zero, zero, nine…

TOM: Nice one.

ALEX: Four, six, seven…

TOM: Don't get distracted.

ALEX completes the rest of the number in silence.

Don't talk about the weather.

ALEX: It's ringing.

Beat.

Baby?… Hi, it's me.

SEVEN

The camp. An interrogation room.

DEMISSIE MULENEH hangs upside down. SYRAH spins him. ALEX enters; seeing DEMISSIE, he hesitates, looks away.

ALEX: *Sorry.*

SYRAH: *You're five minutes late.*

ALEX: *I was trying to call home, sorry. (Turning his back to DEMISSIE.) What would you like me to do?*

SYRAH: *Translate.*

ALEX: *Yes. Where do we start?*

SYRAH spins DEMISSIE.

SYRAH: *Who were you trying to call?*

ALEX: *My wife; couldn't get a signal.*

SYRAH: *No signal on Side Two.*

ALEX: *I know.*

SYRAH: *So why try?*

No answer.

What's your wife's name?

ALEX: *Fiona.*

SYRAH: *How long have you been married?*

ALEX: *…*

SYRAH: *It's a question.*

ALEX: *Are you interrogating me?*

SYRAH: *Are you nervous?*

SYRAH spins DEMISSIE.

Nerves are a good thing. Nice watch.

ALEX: *Gets me from A to B.*

SYRAH: *(Of DEMISSIE.) He's a perfect weight.*

ALEX: *That's what hangmen say.*

SYRAH: *(To DEMISSIE.) What's your name?*

ALEX: *Lieutenant…*

SYRAH: *I'm talking to him. (To DEMISSIE.) I know what it is, but I want you to tell me.*

Pause.

(To DEMISSIE.) Your name's Demissie Muluneh. (To ALEX.) His name's Demissie Muluneh.

ALEX nods. Pause.

(To DEMISSIE.) What do I have to do to make you talk?

No answer.

(To ALEX.) This can go on for days. It's been known to go on for weeks.

ALEX: *How old is he?*

No answer.

What're the allegations against him?

SYRAH: *Why?*

ALEX: *(Shrugs.) Just…*

SYRAH: *Understanding why he's here isn't going to make any difference.*

ALEX: *Isn't it?*

SYRAH: *Why he's here, isn't why we're here.*

ALEX: *We?*

SYRAH: *You and I.*

DEMISSIE mutters.

(To ALEX.) What did he say?

ALEX: *I didn't catch it.*

ALEX leans close to DEMISSIE, who is speaking in a low mumble.

SYRAH: *Don't get too…*

DEMISSIE bites ALEX's ear. ALEX screams. SYRAH drags ALEX away.

Idiot.

ALEX: *Shit.*

SYRAH: *Didn't you learn anything?!*

ALEX: *Shit!*

ALEX stems the blood with a handkerchief. She waits.

Sorry.

SYRAH: *They suck people's eyes out.*

ALEX: *I've only been here two days.*

SYRAH: *So you better fucking learn.*

Beat.

What was he saying?

ALEX: *Fuck you.*

SYRAH: *What?*

ALEX: *He said, 'fuck you'.*

They smile.

SYRAH: *What's your name?*

ALEX: *Lieutenant Brines.*

SYRAH: *First name?*

ALEX: *Alex.*

SYRAH: *You were on Side One?*

ALEX: *Six months, yes. We were told there's been an intensification.*

SYRAH: *'Clear 'em out, bring 'em in.' (Sees his look.) Someone said it should be inscribed somewhere.*

ALEX: *Above the gates maybe.*

SYRAH: *We're not Nazis Lieutenant Brines. It's a phrase; camp humour. What do you think so far?*

ALEX: *We're not exactly hitting it off.*

SYRAH: *Of Side Two.*

ALEX: *It's not how I remembered it.*

SYRAH: *(Smiling.) From the induction day?*

ALEX: *The cell blocks we saw had beds and chairs, there were DVDs and fridges.*

SYRAH: *Soothes enquiring minds.*

ALEX: *Building a show home.*

SYRAH: *Not me personally. But whatever way you look at it, it keeps the doubters happy. You need to get to grips with it.*

ALEX: *I will. What rank are you?*

SYRAH: *I was recruited.*

ALEX: *You're not military.*

    SYRAH spins DEMISSIE.

    So what do I call you?

SYRAH: *(Of DEMISSIE.) He knows me as Helen.*

    Unsure, ALEX says nothing.

ALEX: *How long will you leave him hanging like that?*

    No answer.

    Do you use lie detectors?

    SYRAH watches him.

    How do you know what's useful? I'd just make it up, say anything.

    Silence.

    He's not said a word.

SYRAH: *So we need to be more persistent. How's your ear?*

ALEX: *Better.*

SYRAH: Good. So, let's not waste any more time. What language does he speak? Are you fluent?

ALEX: Amharic. / Perfectly fluent.

SYRAH: I love the way your tongue does that.

She does an rrr sound with her tongue.

Where's it from?

ALEX: It's Semitic, most / commonly found in…

SYRAH: Why translating?

ALEX: I was travelling. I ran out of money and I spent the night at Hanover railway station. I started to read my German dictionary, something to ease the boredom.

SYRAH: And where would I learn to be a translator?

ALEX: Is that what you want to do?

SYRAH: I might. If I can make a sound like that all day, I might. Rrrrrr…

She lifts her skirt and grabs under her knickers.

ALEX: What are you doing?

She produces a bleeding tampon.

SYRAH: Pardon?

ALEX: I said what the / fuck are you…?

SYRAH: Tell this mandog if he doesn't tell me who's financing him that he'll end his days sucking on the crust end of this.

ALEX stares at her.

ALEX: What?

SYRAH: You heard.

ALEX: You're joking.

SYRAH: Tell him. You're here to translate aren't you?!

ALEX: It's a breach / of the…

SYRAH: I don't give a fuck.

ALEX: It's a major / fucking…

SYRAH: Tell him, or I'll do it anyway.

ALEX spins SYRAH round and disarms her of the tampon, sending it to the back of the room.

Idiot.

SYRAH leaves. ALEX is aware of DEMISSIE, still hanging there, watching. He kneels at his side.

ALEX: I…

DEMISSIE spits at him. Instinctively, ALEX raises his hand and hits DEMISSIE in the face.

Bastard.

ALEX watches him, caught by DEMISSIE's stare. He turns to leave.

DEMISSIE: Remember me when you sleep in your bed.

ALEX stops.

Ask yourself who I really am. *(Whispers.)* **Don't let the woman know I was talking. She'll be cross.**

Blackout.

EIGHT

The camp. A DVD messaging suite. ALEX and TOM are present. TOM sits before the screen. ALEX waits, just off, next in the queue. TOM's face is projected large before us.

TOM: September 22nd.

Private Tom Merson.

DVD Message 2.

Alright Mum?

Hope all's spick and span with you. Been here nearly three weeks now isn't it? Missing everyone big time. Can't say one way or the other Mum, to be honest, whether I did a good thing or a bad signing that dotted line. Felt right at the time isn't it?

Mum, are you keeping safe? News daily about bombs. The lads here say they'll run out of idiots daft enough to do it! Talking of idiots, say hello to Bick and Pricey for me? How are they? Pair of mad bastards, isn't it?

Weather's v hot and we have to top up the sun cream on an hourly basis. Our Sarge says when we send messages back, to say we're here to defend yous all back home. So, Mum, are you proud of your son? Tell you what, why don't I get you a ticket and you can come out for the weekend and get a look at some of the dodgy gits who are causing us all so much trouble. Look normal some of them. Like me I think. Sometimes I think they can't decide whether what they've done is a good thing, or a bad thing, too. Sorry. Allegedly. Sarge says we have to keep saying it's 'alleged' that so and so bombed Buck Palace, it's alleged that so and so bombed the Taj Mahal, or whatever.

Anyways, 'all t'world's queer 'cept for theee and me and even theeeee's a bit…' (finish it then!)

Oh yeah, one more weird one. Every morning we have to take a box of rain to their cages. I'm on supply duties. Box of rain? What's that about? No rain I can see isn't it?

A radioed voice interrupts.

VOICE: *You can't say that.*

TOM: *What?*

VOICE: *Box of rain. You can't tell your mum about that. It's classified.*

TOM: *Should I stop?*

VOICE: *It's okay. We'll edit it out.*

TOM waits, the voice doesn't return.

TOM: *Bollocks… Lost my thread now.*

Anyway Mum, got to go, canteen's just opened.

You know me, not shy of my grub isn't it?

Look after everyone.

Big loove Tom x

TOM *turns to go. He sees* ALEX. *He edges past, shares a look with* ALEX, *and leaves, unsure what to say.* ALEX *watches him leave, and takes his seat before the DVD screen.*

Blackout.

NINE

The camp. ALEX, SYRAH, *and the* MAJOR.

MAJOR: *Camp Zero is under the orders of the highest commands that govern the Global Economic Alliance.*

ALEX: *Yes Major.*

MAJOR: *So when you walk into any of the interrogation rooms in this camp, you are there to secure information that will aid us in our mission.*

ALEX: *I understand that. I acted out of frustration.*

MAJOR: *What is the mission?*

ALEX: *And I hit the prisoner. He spat at me, / and I hit him, which I'm sorry for.*

MAJOR: *I asked you what the mission is.*

ALEX: *The mission? As I understand it, our mission sir, is to build relationships with the prisoners / whereby we can…*

SYRAH: *Wrong.*

MAJOR: *And incorrect. The mission, Lieutenant, is to put these people in a court of law whereby they can stand trial for their crimes. To do that we must interrogate them and secure information upon which we can act. With all the will in the world Lieutenant Brines, as Commander of Detainee Operations, I set out to build relationships with anyone who comes through the doors of this camp, and to treat them in as humane a way as possible. To carry out this mission we all have to work together, and what we can't endorse is maverick behaviour.*

ALEX: Smearing that man with blood from a used tampon is maverick beyond the call of duty, sir.

SYRAH: It wasn't real.

ALEX looks at SYRAH.

What do you take me for?

ALEX: Is that supposed to make a difference?

SYRAH: I'm four months pregnant.

MAJOR: Posting out, when?

SYRAH: (Mock annoyance.) *Nine weeks Tuesday, sir.*

MAJOR: Nice.

ALEX: Even if it was a fake, don't you think sir, that tactics of that kind play to our worst instincts?

MAJOR: (Aside to SYRAH.) *I do know when, I just forgot.*

SYRAH: Lieutenant Brines, we're your friends.

ALEX: I was asked to translate, not humiliate.

SYRAH: Nice.

MAJOR: Let's look at the facts.

He takes out a file.

TEN

ALEX stares at the mobile phone.

TOM: *And you asked her isn't it?*

ALEX: **You know I did.**

TOM: **'Should-we-give-ourselves-up?'**

ALEX: **Yeah.**

TOM: **... So what?**

ALEX: **What?**

TOM: **What did she say?**

ALEX: 'No.'

Beat.

TOM: What else?

ALEX: Nothing.

TOM: That's all she said?

ALEX: She said we mustn't give up.

TOM: Give up what?

ALEX: The book…ourselves…

TOM: What else?

ALEX: Nothing else.

TOM: *You were on the phone for twenty fucking minutes, you hardly said a word, what else did she say to you isn't it?*

ALEX: Nothing. Just get the book into safe hands, don't lose a single word of it, don't compromise. If we / hand over the book then…

TOM: Fuck. Isn't it? *Then what?* What did she say? *If we hand over the book then what?*

ALEX: Then nothing. There isn't a 'then what'. We've got no other choice, we've got to see it through.

TOM dives for the envelope and ALEX snatches it away, moving to the other side of the room.

TOM: *I'll fucking swing for you man…*

ALEX: (Dodging TOM.) That's not / a good idea.

TOM: *I don't need to be here isn't it, I've been tricked, I've been fucking tricked…!!*

TOM gives up, and lies flat out, desperate, breathless. ALEX stares at the book in the envelope. Silence, until…

ALEX: (Not unsympathetic to TOM's cause.) Anyway, just think of the money you're going to make from all this.

TOM: (Face in the pillow.) I never thought I'd hear myself say this, but right now I don't give a fuck about money isn't it? I want something soft. In my life.

I want softness.

All of a sudden.

Beat.

ALEX: And you want coffee.

TOM looks at ALEX.

ELEVEN

The camp. ALEX, SYRAH, and the MAJOR, continued. SYRAH hands a cup of coffee to the MAJOR, he sips it.

MAJOR: *This guy.*

SYRAH: *Major?*

MAJOR: *The tampon guy.*

SYRAH: *Sir.*

MAJOR: *What's his name?*

SYRAH: *(Peering at the file.) Demiss…Dennis…somethingorrother.*

ALEX: *Demissie.*

SYRAH: *(To the MAJOR.) Coffee?*

MAJOR: *Right. So this Demissie…*

As ALEX continues, SYRAH exits and returns with a mug of coffee that she hands to the MAJOR.

ALEX: *Can I be dismissed sir?*

MAJOR: *No.*

ALEX: *I'd really like to leave the room.*

MAJOR: *You'll leave when I'm ready. According to the information in these files Demissie Mulunuh…/*

ALEX: *The pronunciation is Mulen-eh, sir.*

MAJOR: Purchased six types of plastic explosive, online, in a four-week period, using three different credit cards, under four assumed identities, at six different times of the day. Do you relish the recording, analysing, and ultimate long term prohibition of such permutations as these Brines?

ALEX: No sir. Major, I understand the concerns we should have about some of the people in this camp, but consciously allowing this kind of interrogation offers us no advantage.

SYRAH: (To the MAJOR, by way of mock explanation.) It's bad for our image.

MAJOR: Such profundity in abandon Brines. The tampon incident was the tip of an iceberg, and your concerns for the torture tactics utilised in this camp transport me back in time Lieutenant. Twenty years ago it was your kind of bullshit, liberalist rhetoric that never allowed places like Guantanamo Bay to become the ballbreaker it should have been. And so it's my job as commanding officer of Detainee Operations to do what?

ALEX: Maintain discipline sir.

MAJOR: And focus Brines. Across the globe, reported attacks on innocent citizens are currently clocking in at **one** *every* **two** *hours. Night and day. In the most far-flung places you can look and you can find a plan, a detail, an idea for reducing people to dust. Yes? No? Read the data Brines, the world's most senior sociologists now acknowledge that we are living through a feast of unabated avarice, a desire for wealth that outweighs past disagreements as prosaic as East versus / West, or left versus…*

ALEX: I do understand this sir.

MAJOR: Good. So you know that to walk down the street, any street in the world, is a risk to one's personal safety.

ALEX: Yes sir.

SYRAH: Good. So the right, therefore, to enforce enhanced interrogation techniques is the business of any fair-minded patriot Lieutenant Brines.

ALEX: Yes ma'am.

MAJOR: I'm glad you mentioned that.

SYRAH: *Sir?*

MAJOR: *Patriotism.*

ALEX: *May I be dismissed sir?*

MAJOR: *No. I haven't finished with Demissie Muleneh. I want you to imagine Brines, that Muleneh's internet shopping spree for bomb-making materials is complete, and he decides that he'll make six dirty bombs and plant them all over the island of…Majorca. How many people live in Majorca, Lieutenant Brines?*

ALEX: *I've not been sir.*

SYRAH: *It's beautiful.*

MAJOR: *Or maybe Beijing? Harare, Manhattan, Caracas? How many people would die?*

ALEX: *That's impossible to calculate sir.*

MAJOR: *And one hour before the bombs are due to go off we're lucky enough to catch him. But he won't talk for God's sake, he won't tell us where the bombs are. Do we sit around and remind ourselves of his human rights? 'I'm afraid Mr Muleneh won't talk, so we'll have to let several thousand innocent people die.' Or instead Lieutenant, we can use other methods designed to make Mr Muleneh talk, and give us the information we need.*

ALEX: *But* **Sir***… (Calmer.) Major, I've been standing in an interrogation room for the best part of a fortnight, watching… (Gestures to SYRAH.) Helen, or some other such person, torturing men and women who have been held here for months, in some cases years. I know about torture, it happens, I'm not naive…*

SYRAH: *No.*

ALEX: *But standing there, face to face, someone telling me it's my* **job** *to… (Laughs.) I will* **not** *associate myself with such…*

MAJOR: *You'll do / as you are ordered Lieutenant.*

ALEX: *If some of these detainees… It occurred to me…if some of these people, it seems so obvious sir, if some of them* **are** *connected to attempts to plant dirty bombs, or* **might** *possess a list of associates, do you really believe that the trail is still going to be hot, / or that…*

MAJOR: The military possess many brilliant minds Lieutenant. It's not like it hasn't occurred to us. But like you, we follow the orders that are given to us. Those that don't follow their orders have often found themselves re-deployed.

ALEX: So I'm not the only one thinking this sir.

MAJOR: I've always believed in being open Brines, and I'd be lying to you if I didn't admit that others have stood before me in the same way as you do now. But like I said, those that don't follow their orders have often found themselves re-deployed. Have I made that clear enough for you, or should I spell it out?

Beat.

SYRAH: I suggest you tell the Major, in the instance of his Majorca scenario, what the appropriate course of action would be.

ALEX: Neither choice seems straightforward ma'am.

MAJOR: Well I'm interested by the idea that you think we have a choice Lieutenant. What we're stood in this room debating is the politics of fucking envy Brines.

ALEX: Yes sir.

*MAJOR: 'He has more than me, therefore I will kill him.' Not always fact, but perception. The Others detained here in Camp Zero are unremittingly pissed off, would you agree? Why? Because The Others are people who have no other aspirations but to be **rich** for Christ's sake, they've **worked, all their lives**, to afford the pleasures of wealth…*

ALEX: I understand this also sir.

*MAJOR: Good. Better houses, better health, faster cars, and because, no matter how much they try, they will never feel that they are as rich as we are, because, in contrast to us they feel **poor**, The Others have decided to take us out. QED. This is hatred unleashed for no other ideological purpose than the thrill of destruction, revenge that climbs on the back of any old fucking nationality, and doesn't give a fuck who it hurts. Response, Lieutenant?*

ALEX: Protect our assets sir.

The MAJOR goes back to his desk.

MAJOR: *For all your misgivings Lieutenant, if you think we can tackle people as disaffected and as widespread as these with the Geneva Dementia around our necks, if you think perhaps we have a choice in the face of such brutal premeditation, then you're out of here.*

ALEX: *Yes please.*

MAJOR: *What?*

ALEX: *Post me somewhere else.*

MAJOR: *To Camp Two perhaps. Or Camp Three. What about Camp Four, or five? Perhaps Camp four hundred and twenty-seven?*

ALEX: *Sir?*

MAJOR: *Currently, there are five hundred and twenty-six camps of this kind in existence.*

ALEX looks shocked.

(To SYRAH.) He's actually quite entertaining. (To ALEX.) Camps on planes, Brines. Huge airliners endlessly traversing the globe, camps on ships, underground, camps in the Mojave desert, the Sahara and the Outback. Camps in the Lake District, Provence, Languedoc, camps being built in Bavaria, Macedonia, camps under construction on both the North and South Islands of New Zealand, camps almost complete in the Newfoundland and Manitoba regions of Canada, camps finished only last week, three of them in the Chinese provinces of Shandong, Hainan, and Jaingsu, camps in the central belts of Russia, camps in the heart of Sao Paulo and Lima. Camps across the world all armed with the same mission: to get the information we need to save our fucked-up skins.

SYRAH: *'Who finances you? Who organises you? Who arms you? And who harbours you?'*

The MAJOR closes the file.

MAJOR: *If you think you can control the use of tampons in all of these camps then you have a good go, and shout it out loud and fucking proud. Shout it, and wait for the bullet. Back of the head. Because it's not very popular Brines, defending the rights of a terrorist. (Beat.) Dismissed.*

Lights.

TWELVE

Night. ALEX stands alone watching DEMISSIE, who is in his cage. Aware he is being watched, DEMISSIE turns and looks at ALEX. They stare, wait. Until…

ALEX: *…I'm sorry I hit you.*

Silence.

Why did you say that to me… 'remember me when you sleep in your bed'…

No answer.

Why would I be bothered…?

DEMISSIE raises his eyebrows.

I didn't mean it like that… I meant… I'm saying, you can see I'm not part of any of this… In those rooms, you can see I'm not…that I don't believe in what they do to you…

Silence

…Of course I'll remember you. But not with guilt…not with…

Silence.

Don't judge me. (He stops.) But you're not listening anyway. Why should you?

DEMISSIE looks a little longer at ALEX, and turns away.

THIRTEEN

The camp. TOM and ALEX stand at the edge of the compound, as before.

TOM: *Not smoking?*

No answer.

Not seen you for a few days isn't it?

ALEX: Busy.

TOM: Plenty of people needing translating.

ALEX: I can't say too much.

TOM: Course you can't. Watch what you say here isn't it? Don't say that plate of fish and chips was very nice thanks very much. Might mean something, might reveal something.

ALEX: Fish and chips?

TOM: I thought I was joining up to defend, not be a robot...

ALEX: (Without enthusiasm.) Try and remember you're talking to an officer.

TOM: Yes sir. 'Cept you've got a face as long as my knob isn't it? Look like you could do with a chat.

ALEX: You don't want to know.

TOM: Like I don't understand?

ALEX: No.

TOM: Yeah. Isn't it? Tension's like a fart waiting to burst in this place isn't it? Tell me, and I'll tell you, yeah? You know what I'm saying?... Like, okay... I don't know if you've thought about it, but most of the prisoners here got that death warmed up look sir isn't it?

ALEX laughs.

Just wondering isn't it? I want revenge, but we're civilised isn't it?

ALEX smiles.

What? Young boy I heard about, been here 18 months, no lawyer, Bolivian or something. He got stopped at La Paz airport 'cos of the colour of his bag. They said it was significant. Last week, had the fuck beaten out of him three days on the trot isn't it? Fucking arm's broken and no one's... It's just...

TOM demonstrates, hangs his arm limp and twisted. ALEX laughs again.

Fuck this, not standing round for you to take the piss out / of me isn't it!

ALEX: *Come / here.*

TOM: *Fuck off…*

ALEX: *Private.*

TOM *stops. Turns back to face ALEX.*

I know. (Pause. Again.) I know.

TOM: *Isn't it?*

ALEX *nods.*

What is this place exactly?

No answer.

End of the day, do my job though isn't it? Don't get involved. (Checks his watch.) Off for a beer sir.

ALEX: *My first name's Alex.*

TOM: *Cool.*

FOURTEEN

The camp. SYRAH and ALEX are present at the continued interrogation and torture of DEMISSIE, who is hung upside down as before. He has been soaked with drugs that loosen his mind and tongue. He speaks not only to himself, but to a vision of his wife.

As DEMISSIE speaks, SYRAH talks to ALEX and prepares a series of scalpels and blades on a roll-out cloth. ALEX watches from the back of the room.

DEMISSIE: *…star…sweet… See…? Sweet soul…and can I touch you…?…come and sit…here…here star…my arms, star, see…? Needles and holes… This needle, this hole they put in Demissie and I'm… (He laughs.) I've been, I've been…I've… been…yes and I have, I have, I've…been…I've…I've…rrrggg… ffhdrgfttph…*

SYRAH: *The drugs instigate the Contradictory Comparison. Large streams of narrative, followed by a series of stumblings; the words are forced to stick and corrupt. Don't let that put you off, just tell me everything he says. It won't make sense for a time, but tell me anyway.*

Silence.

It helps if you at least acknowledge that you've understood my instructions.

ALEX nods. She continues lining up needles and phials on the table.

I saw you last night.

ALEX watches her.

Three in the morning. Wandering the perimeter fence.

ALEX: *(Of* DEMISSIE.*) Is he thirsty?*

SYRAH: *Sleeping can be difficult.*

ALEX: *I'll give him some water.*

SYRAH: *Not until I say. (Holds up a needle.) One brisk circuit of the camp, that's all I need. Shake off the cobwebs. Give the baby a work out.*

ALEX: *(Looking to her belly.) Don't you find it strange?*

SYRAH: *Pregnancy is natural Lieutenant, / didn't anyone teach you about the…*

ALEX: *You know what I mean.*

SYRAH: *My child's the most important thing in the world to me. Any mother should be prepared to do whatever it takes. Any father for that matter. Do you have kids?*

ALEX: *Not yet.*

SYRAH: *Plans though. The strength of the alliance defends my rights, and my child's rights to live without fear. Don't you want to live without fear?*

ALEX: *You sound like Major Chaudry.*

SYRAH: *I can think for myself.*

ALEX: Right.

SYRAH: Six years ago I was a practising psychologist. I resisted, much like you are now. I watched the world imploding, unravelling. And I listened every day for weeks on end to the stories of people sent to me for treatment. Queues outside the door, queues of zombies welled up with fear so massed that they could barely breathe. What treatment could I offer them from behind a desk? If the world is mad, which it surely is, then this is the best treatment I can offer.

SYRAH considers DEMISSIE and takes a bottle of water to him. She pours it into his mouth, gentle, concentrated, like with a newborn. She wipes it from his mouth.

DEMISSIE: Lying... I'm lying with you... I'm lying... Star...see...? why's this, this, this, this this / this this...

SYRAH: What's he saying?

DEMISSIE: But I remember the afternoon...sweet soul, see...?

SYRAH: What's he saying?

DEMISSIE: And I remember the afternoon...happy...

SYRAH: Lieutenant.

DEMISSIE: The afternoon...sweet soul, didn't we cry, like I cry... now...

SYRAH: Lieutenant Brines.

DEMISSIE: Hear our baby's cry, and didn't we, because there was... and so much...

He mumbles.

SYRAH: Well?

ALEX: Happiness. He said something about happiness.

SYRAH: It's helpful if you tell me what he's saying.

DEMISSIE: ...we were stars, and you are my star and we were stars...and I caught you...

SYRAH: What's he saying now?

ALEX shrugs.

DEMISSIE: You fell and I caught you, can't be caught by / those tears star...

SYRAH: Fuck's sake.

DEMISSIE: The cry from baby...remember / the cry from baby...

SYRAH: Tell me exactly what he's saying.

DEMISSIE: From our baby star...and the / best day...

ALEX: Just...

DEMISSIE: Best, best, life is...can't change it when life is...life is life, and life is...it's...see...?

> Out of patience, SYRAH picks up a phial of drugs and a needle and moves towards DEMISSIE.

SYRAH: Right.

ALEX: He's just muttering alright? It's nothing, it's... Stuff about his family, about how happy he was when their child was born.

SYRAH: So he has children?

ALEX: He must have.

> SYRAH goes back to the table. She puts down the phial and needle, and picks up a scalpel. She wipes it with a cloth.

> *So what are you doing?*

> ALEX is fixated, watching SYRAH as she approaches DEMISSIE, scalpel in hand. ALEX moves to SYRAH.

> *Look, for Christ's sake...*

> SYRAH lifts the scalpel in his direction. He stops. She waits, and then turns back to DEMISSIE.

FIFTEEN

The camp. ALEX sits in silence; withdrawn, aimless.

A helicopter lifts away.

TOM passes, he carries a box of rain.

TOM: *Alright sir?... Woah!* (Of the helicopter.) *Lucky bastards. On their way home!*

TOM's walkie talkie crackles. A voice is heard.

VOICE: *Rain Detail, are you reading me? Over.*

TOM: (To ALEX.) *Just a sec sir.* (Into walkie-talkie.) *Yeah, reading.*

VOICE: *Are you on your way to 352? Over.*

TOM: (Into walkie-talkie.) *En route. Over.*

VOICE: *Don't bother, he's gone.*

TOM: (Into walkie-talkie.) *Right.*

VOICE: *Ditto 355 and 358. Over.*

TOM: (Into walkie-talkie.) *They're all gone, yeah? Okay. Over.*

A second helicopter lifts away.

Watch your head sir!! (Of the choppers.) *That'll be us in six months.*

TOM laughs ironically, like six months is something to really celebrate.

Cheer up sir, s'like squeezing shit out of a lemon isn't it?

No answer.

Better get this box back anyways.

The sound of a car, but at high pitch, its engine screaming and shouts and cheers of excitement. They watch it pass.

Hey! That's the lads heading down the waste ground. You want a go on the jeep?

ALEX looks at him.

Isn't it?! Cos if you fall off and die, it's my fault, you got me?! (Calls.) *Hey! Dickheads! I'm off duty in ten, get that roof ready for me isn't it!!* (Back to ALEX.) *Oh yeah, can't call me private no more either, been made Corporal.*

ALEX: *Congratulations.*

TOM: *Yesterday isn't it? And tomorrow I'm volunteering. You know the presidents are visiting? The Initial Reaction Force got to do a demonstration, they asked me to help out. Drive you mad, but you can get on in a place like this isn't it? Respect. Promotions.*

TOM heads off.

Keep it easy sir, isn't it?

The jeep powers up and there is the screeching sound of its engine.

SIXTEEN

The camp. A DVD/video messaging booth. ALEX sits before a camera.

ALEX: *October 31st*

Lieutenant Alex Brines.

DVD message 7

Hiya…

ALEX stops as soon as he starts, staring forlornly into the camera. He rouses himself.

I love you.

I'm sick…

Nothing's changed.

Shakes his head.

It's worse.

And I'm there, I'm… These rooms. Night, day. No windows. Listening. Watching.

… Am I?

My eyes don't belong to me. Not any more.

It's what I've learned.

And the Major says, every day, I must translate.

And they keep…they use me, eight, ten, twelve hours…

Strange conversation, this morning. Officer stopped me in the mess. He said I'd been nominated for a pay rise. Did I want it? The pay rise is huge, beyond our dreams and I think I understand what he was doing.

Isn't money and oblivion so tempting baby?

Where did I go?

To.

He stops. Starts again.

Rape, amputation…

I've… Seen.

I've…

A radioed voice interrupts.

VOICE: *Stop.*

ALEX: *What?*

VOICE: *You can't include these things in your message.*

ALEX: *It's supposed to be personal.*

VOICE: *You know the drill.*

ALEX: *I don't care about the drill!!… Fuck's sake, I've seen these things happening, I've seen it here in the camp…*

VOICE: *Message finished.*

The screen goes black and the camera shuts down.

ALEX: *Turn it back on!! I was speaking…*

Nothing happens.

Turn it back on!!

The screen stays dark. ALEX waits, waits, his head lowered. Finally, he looks vacantly at his watch. Silence. He stands, leaves.

SEVENTEEN

The hideout. Night. ALEX stares at TOM.

TOM: (Slow, angry patience.) You spoke to your wife on the phone for *twenty* fucking minutes. I sat and I waited twenty fucking minutes, and all you tell me is that she said we shouldn't give up the book. Isn't it? Crap man, frankly. My head's spinning, I'm feeling like I don't exist, / and you won't even…

ALEX: So go to sleep.

TOM: What?

ALEX: You heard.

TOM: Stuck up bastard.

ALEX: Yeah.

TOM: Wanker.

ALEX: Yeah.

TOM: Think you're better than me 'cos you wrote a book?

ALEX: I could've…*all this,* I could've told anyone in that camp, but I told you, I told you / because…

TOM: Because I got beaten up. Convenient isn't it?

ALEX: Because you were crying… You came to see me and you broke down, and in that…*shit* hole, I held you.

TOM goes to the window. An exasperated silence. Until…

TOM: I've got a number.

ALEX: For what?

TOM: On the ship. You were sleeping, and I rang the Defence Department at the Global Economic Alliance.

ALEX: Jesus.

TOM: You wouldn't believe it, got straight through. I spoke to some guy, told him we were sorry for leaving like we did,

but we didn't want to spend all our life on the run, and he says, 'Sorry about what?'

ALEX: **What do you mean?**

TOM: **And then I told him about the book.**

The voice on the end of the phone line is heard.

VOICE: What book?

TOM: Just a… Is this alright? Can I talk to you in private?

VOICE: There's no one else listening.

TOM: Lieutenant Brines wrote a book about Camp Zero. He's got it all in there, torture, interrogation techniques, what you people do, what you people did to **me***!*

VOICE: You?

TOM: ME!! Yeah! (TOM goes mental.) LAZY FUCKING LAYABOUT SMART ARSED UP YOUR OWN ARSE WANKERS WHO THINK YOU'RE BETTER THAN EVERYONE ELSE, THAT YOU CAN DO WHATEVER THE FUCK YOU WANT TO WHOEVER THE FUCK YOU PLEASE…!!!

Silence.

Hello…? Sorry about that, I just…

VOICE: Wait a second.

ALEX: **How stupid are you?**

TOM: **I thought they'd…**

The voice is heard again on the end of the phone line.

VOICE: I don't need to tell you how stupid you've been.

TOM: Not just me, Lieutenant Brines as well.

VOICE: Where are you?

TOM: What?… Why do you need to know that?

VOICE: Where are you?

TOM: *(Bottling it.) I erm... Listen, I think I've fucked up actually isn't it?*

VOICE: *I'm going to give you a number.*

TOM: *No.*

VOICE: *Memorise it. 0054 780002 4678*

TOM: *Okay.*

VOICE: *0000502476004040000. Got it?*

TOM: *(Unsure.) I think so, can I just...*

VOICE: *Take some time. Think it through. Make the right decision. And call us.*

TOM: *When? When do I have to call...?*

The line clicks out, and is replaced by an automated voice.

VOICE: *This is the Global Economic Alliance, Department of:... Defence. Press 1 for emergencies, press 2 for tactical advice, press 3 for...*

TOM **hangs up. He stares at** ALEX.

TOM: **The right decision. It's all I can think about, cos if we make the right decision then we might...do you know what I'm saying isn't it? I can ring him now, tell him we've got the book, and we can arrange for him to pick it up.**

ALEX: **Idiot.**

TOM: **Just give me the mobile.**

ALEX: **I flushed it down the toilet. When I was in there and you said 'what're you doing' and I said I was being sick, I flushed it down the toilet.**

TOM: **That's my** *phone!*

ALEX: **I know.**

TOM **goes to the bathroom.**

TOM: **Urghh... Animal, you're a fucking...! (Off.) It's gone...** *it's fucking...* **Got another 12 months on that!**

TOM comes back into the room, his hand dripping wet. ALEX has had the phone all the time. He holds it out for TOM.

You think I'm one big joke isn't it?

TOM goes to his bag, starts packing.

ALEX: You'll be on your own.

TOM: At one with nature. Lovely.

ALEX: The last hundred miles was bush, / it was just...

TOM: So I'll walk.

ALEX: You go out there and call some guy...

TOM: I will.

ALEX: What?

TOM: I'm going to.

ALEX: *What?*

TOM: You just said, 'you got out there and call some guy...'

ALEX: Stop fucking about.

TOM: I'm not / fucking about.

ALEX: I meant, if you *call* him then we're... Fuck's sake, you *know* what I meant. *Listen.* Okay, so they know about the book, and I *was,* you're right. I was on the phone to my wife for twenty minutes and I'm sorry, I didn't mean to make you feel... *but it was twenty minutes of pure fucking inspiration, so personal, so...* I tell her about the book and what me and you decided to do, and she's talking to me like I'm a God... Flatlining Tom, *all my life,* doing the minimum fucking amount... And now this happens to me, and she's talking to me like I'm a *GOD,* like I've got all the knowledge in all the world, she loves me, she wants me home, but she says she never thought I could do something like this, she's so proud of me, she's...

TOM: She's getting off on it, yeah?

ALEX: ...and she says publishing the book, maybe in the scheme of things no one'll care, but for the *idea* to grow in me, for the passion, to grow...*passion*, she says, *conscience*, she says, that's...

TOM: She sounds totally fucking horny by the way, the way she talks, isn't it?

ALEX: And part of me, I know I'm an idiot...to think I can make a difference by writing a book, it's *ideals*, it's... I DIDN'T GO LOOKING FOR THIS TOM...but she's right, isn't she?... It's not just for me, it's for you, it's for *everyone*, because people need to know the truth. Where can you find the truth? These days. (He waits.) You leave here, you call that guy and tell him we're giving up the book, then it won't end there. You'll have to deliver it.

TOM: He didn't say that.

ALEX: But that's next. When you ring, he'll say you have to deliver it. And then you're in their hands.

TOM: Yeah, and clean. Drinking coffee. They're not all bad you know.

ALEX: Fine. And after that they'll probably torture you.

TOM stops packing.

You don't want that again. Their torture. Do you? I remember your pain. I remember what they did to you.

TOM stares at ALEX. He punches him in the face.

Blackout.

EIGHTEEN

The camp. TOM is dragged into the space and the MAJOR and SOLDIER 1 truss up his ankles with ropes, blindfold him, and place shackles on his hands, behind his back.

MAJOR: *Presidents, can I thank you for your patience. My name is Major Chaudry. Today, you will witness a re-enactment of the procedures utilised within our Initial Reaction Force, here at*

Camp Zero. We will conduct the exercise in English, it being our common language, but should there be any translation issues Lieutenant Brines is here to assist. To begin then, the hands, as you can see, are shackled and placed as tightly to the body of the prisoner as possible. Tighter please.

We can see TOM's immediate discomfort.

I should point out that the person here before you today isn't a detainee, that would be completely unethical, but a private serving here at the camp.

TOM: *Corporal.*

MAJOR: *As a mark of the commitment we enjoy from those serving at Camp Zero, this man has offered himself as a volunteer for the purposes of our demonstration.*

TOM: *Corporal.*

MAJOR: *Pardon?*

TOM: *Just been promoted to a Corporal, isn't it?*

Beat.

MAJOR: *Sirs, if you can imagine an incident in one of the cages, perhaps an attack on one of the guards, or an attempt at either suicide or escape, then the Initial Reaction Force will respond to an alarm which is heard across the entire camp.*

The sound of an alarm.

Following the alarm, the IRF descend on the relevant cage, seize the prisoner and bring them from the cage compound to this room… Documentation is crucial for legal purposes. Initial Reaction Force: pose one.

SOLDIER 1 twists TOM round, posing him grotesquely for a camera that the MAJOR holds. The latter takes a photo of TOM.

SOLDIER 1: *Sir!*

MAJOR: *Initial Reaction Force: pose two.*

Same again with the camera

SOLDIER 1: *Sir!*

MAJOR: Burn it. Archive it.

SOLDIER 1: Sir!

MAJOR: Make sure I get a copy.

SOLDIER 1: Sir!

MAJOR: The detainee will be restrained and bound, as you have watched, and hoisted…

SOLDIER 1 grabs the rope and hoists TOM up, so that he hangs upside down.

Into the air. It looks uncomfortable, but at least now the detainee is going nowhere, and we can proceed in a manner which we feel enables the detainee to understand how unhappy we are. Hit pressure point one.

SOLDIER 1 hits TOM, and TOM screams in pain.

Hit pressure point two.

SOLDIER 1 hits TOM, and he screams in pain.

And start.

SOLDIER 1 starts to hit TOM repeatedly, and he screams in pain under the barrage of violence.

SOLDIER 1: You are not subject to the laws of the Geneva Convention, or any of the conditions attached thereof. You are a prisoner not of conscience, but of violence. You have bombed, and maimed. You are subject to the rules of torture under the agreement of the Global Economic Alliance. You have broken the rules laid out for you on your arrival at the camp, you will be broken, your only hope will be to sip from a single box of rain, left at the door of your cage, to quench your thirst in the barren endlessness of your capture, here, at the camp.

TOM: Stop!! Please!!!!

SOLDIER 1: (To the MAJOR.) The fucker needs breaking.

MAJOR: Just follow the procedure.

SOLDIER 1 hits TOM. He screams in agony. Now he is hitting randomly, beyond procedure.

TOM: *No one said / this would happen!!*

MAJOR: *(To SOLDIER 1, so as not to be heard.)* **I said follow the procedure.**

SOLDIER 1: *I want to break him.*

TOM: *You said it was an exercise.*

ALEX: *(To the MAJOR.)* **You better get him down.**

SOLDIER 1 continues to hit TOM who screams in agony.

TOM: *You said I was taking part in an exercise.*

SOLDIER 1: *I want…*

TOM: *Help me!!!!!!*

ALEX: *He's not a prisoner for God's sake.*

ALEX goes to TOM.

MAJOR: *(To ALEX.)* **I'll deal with this.** *(To SOLDIER 1, so as not to be heard.)* **Follow the procedure.**

SOLDIER 1 ignores the MAJOR, looking instead to where the presidents sit.

SOLDIER 1: *(To ALEX.)* **Impress them.**

TOM: *You're breaking / my fucking bones!!…*

SOLDIER 1: *The presidents are here. Impress them.* *(To ALEX.)* **Hit him, help me hit him.**

ALEX: *What the fuck're you talking about!!? Major, / stop this now…*

MAJOR: *Get back into / position.*

ALEX: *Get him down.*

TOM: *You can't do this to me!!!!!!!!*

MAJOR: *(To ALEX.)* **Get back into position.**

SOLDIER 1 hits TOM again and again, and TOM screams.

SOLDIER 1: *(To ALEX)* **Help me hit him!**

ALEX pulls away from SOLDIER 1, trying to get to TOM. The SOLDIER pushes ALEX away, hits TOM twice more, and then stops, out of breath.

I think that's enough sir.

MAJOR: *(Giving SOLDIER 1 daggers.)* **Thank you soldier.** *(To ALEX. Icy.)* **Thank you Brines, you're dismissed.** *(Back to the Leaders.)* **And so, although perhaps at times a little over zealously, we have, I believe, ably demonstrated the concise and effective powers of the Initial Reaction Force deployed here at Camp Zero.**

SOLDIER 1: **He'll be unconscious in three seconds.**

The two men look at each other, at TOM. As the three seconds end, TOM blacks out.

NINETEEN

The camp. ALEX enters in the darkness, he moves slowly, a torch in his hand, shining it into a series of cages as he crosses the compound. They are all empty. He arrives at the side of DEMISSIE's cage, who wakes with a start.

Silence.

ALEX: *I didn't mean to wake you.*

Silence.

Nightmares.

Long silence.

DEMISSIE: *What do you want?*

Silence.

So you should go away.

TWENTY

The hideout. ALEX holds a shirt to his bloodied nose. TOM lies out on the bed, his eyes closed.

ALEX: (Quietly.) I'm an officer, and you assaulted me.

He checks his nose, gingerly.

Assaulting an officer is an offence.

TOM: Not now isn't it? No more 'Sirs'. You're just Alex, and I'm just Tom, sat out here in the middle of nowhere. Stinking away in our own fucking cage now isn't it?

ALEX: It's got a toilet.

TOM: (Ironic.) More than you get at The Zero.

ALEX: It's the prisoners got us in this shit in the first place.

TOM: Bad workman blames his tools isn't it? Those guys, those *skeletons* back there in their cages, you really think they give a fuck you wrote a book about them?

ALEX: Most of them hate me.

TOM: You live inside the Alliance; they don't. Simple isn't it?

ALEX stands at the window.

Sir, your first words to me; don't get involved isn't it? We're soldiers, our army acts like a bunch of wankers, but what can we do?

Beat.

ALEX: Put things straight.

TWENTY-ONE

The camp. ALEX is at DEMISSIE's cage. DEMISSIE regards him.

DEMISSIE: *Two nights in a row.*

Silence.

Should I be flattered?

ALEX: *You asked me what I wanted.*

DEMISSIE: And last night you had your chance to speak. Things move fast; in here. (Taps his forehead.) The mind mimics the habits of an ocean; washes in, washes out. Nothing remains.

ALEX: If you'll listen.

DEMISSIE: Go away.

Silence.

ALEX: Tomorrow they're resuming your questioning.

Silence.

I have to be there.

DEMISSIE: Leave the room.

ALEX: I'm a serving officer.

DEMISSIE: Serve no one but yourself.

ALEX: I… If you've got…a story, a fiction of some kind, then you should speak that and I'll translate it. It doesn't have to make sense, but you'll have given them something, and then it's done, it's…

DEMISSIE: They'll leave me alone.

ALEX: I…

Silence.

DEMISSIE: Your name's Alex.

ALEX: Yes.

DEMISSIE: You'll have noticed, in my interrogations, that I am prepared to die in silence. None of my life has the luxury of fiction. If you can't understand that, then how can you understand why I acted in the way I did?

ALEX: I took this camp for granted. In the mornings I wake with dread. Whether you're a terrorist or not, has become irrelevant.

DEMISSIE: So we cannot have a conversation. Do something useful, and tell me where the men are who were in this section with me.

ALEX: I don't know.

DEMISSIE: Are they alive, or dead?

ALEX: I can find out.

DEMISSIE: And bring me a new box of rain.

ALEX shoots DEMISSIE a look.

What else should I do but take advantage of you?

ALEX: The rain isn't that easy.

DEMISSIE: If you want to help me.

ALEX: There's a boat, in the harbour. You wouldn't have seen it. Every evening the boat sprays a jet stream into a reservoir. It's not rain. There's no rain on an island like this. It's a Chinese ship, and they have a contract. The rain's sold to us, and a gang of men, they have a supply of boxes like these, and it's their job to box the 'rain', and wrap it ready for delivery to the cages in the morning. I can't get you another box because they'll be preparing them.

DEMISSIE: You're like all the rest.

ALEX: I'd be seen.

DEMISSIE: Go away.

ALEX: I thought we could talk. I… Who are you?

DEMISSIE: You know my name.

ALEX: I'm trying to help you. If I'm caught here I'll be in serious trouble, I've made a big enough nuisance of myself already.

DEMISSIE: My opinion of you should count?

ALEX: Most of my days, they're spent… I'm looking into YOUR eyes… I'm a translator, words are my bread and butter, and you stare back at me, you're silent, you're fucking…and you let her cut you, burn you…she… Fuck's sake, if she tortures you, then you torture me… Don't put me through this any more.

ALEX loses energy. Stops.

It sounds simplistic.

DEMISSIE: Selfish even.

ALEX: Yes.

DEMISSIE: Even if it was more complex, my silence would remain.
(Beat.) But I will speak.

ALEX: Thank you.

DEMISSIE: But only with you now. I'll tell you my story. And then
tomorrow, when she tortures me, and I remain silent, it will hurt
you all the more.

ALEX: That's vile.

DEMISSIE: Yes. Lately, I feel I am more and more vile. Poisoned,
perhaps. But not always. In a different life I have been, or was...
pleasant, hard working. I owned a garage, I fixed the vehicles of
all the diplomats in the city. Fifteen years of my life, and plans for
more garages. Plans to become a 'Business Man'. Three years ago,
the Embassy announced that its work would be put out to tender,
and they gave the contract to a foreign company. My tender was
cheaper, but this company's business was well known, they have
their headquarters in the city, they own oil, and water, and other
utilities over a huge region of the country.

ALEX: Economics, / it's...

DEMISSIE: Yes. And I'm laughed at when I try to tell people that
I can fix the cars as well as this company. Since when did they
care about cars? I am a native of the city, and this company is
foreign, coming and going as it pleases. But it's garages are plush,
they're new. I approach people in the street who look important,
and I try to persuade them to bring their cars to me. They ask for
a card. I say I don't have one. They ask for my website address,
I say I don't have one. But I understand that I need one, that to
compete with this company I should buy my clothes from Paris,
or my shoes from London, and I don't have the money. All my
life, money invades my dreams, hallucinates me, it takes away my
reason because I know I will gladly kiss the feet of The Rich if it
means I too can be like them. And now, just to survive, I realise I
need more money than I ever could imagine. What has happened
to Demissie? My wife is offered work at the Embassy; she works in
the kitchens, what little she earns keeps us afloat, and I continue
with my efforts to bring business back to my garage. I decide to
buy new equipment, but the bank won't give me money. By the
end of the day, I understand that I am alone, and when you are

alone, it is easier to act alone. Friends I talked to before, many had experiences like mine, they were angry, they talked of action. Listening to them, I was unsure. But now I borrow money from a back street loan agency, and I buy explosives and guns from the internet.

ALEX: *Why didn't you use it to buy the new equipment you needed?*

DEMISSIE *stops, he smiles.*

DEMISSIE: *I'm not sure what I will do with these new toys, but I feel a satisfaction in my belly, that I have done something. At the Embassy, my wife works on an important party, and at the end of the night she is stopped at the embassy gates as she leaves with a bag of food that was left uneaten. She explains that her supervisor said to take the food home, but the Embassy's guards say she stole it.*

ALEX: *Did she?*

DEMISSIE: *Why would my wife steal?*

No answer.

The guards laugh and they make her watch as they throw the food to their dogs. It was difficult to sleep. I was haunted by the truth of what it meant for us to have become so worthless, that the Embassy's dogs were better fed than my family. One week after, the company who won the tender had too much work, and one of the diplomats for the Embassy came back to my garage. I put a bomb under his car, and one hour later it detonated and killed him.

ALEX: *Why did you kill him, he was / innocent, he…*

DEMISSIE: *In / some ways…*

ALEX: *Why not bomb the company, they're / the ones who…*

DEMISSIE: *If you have any ideas how to get close to them, please / let me know.*

ALEX: *The work that diplomat brought you was an opportunity to make money, to re-build your reputation.*

DEMISSIE: Yes. And as I stared at his car, I was reminded of the food and the guards and their dogs. What man wouldn't choose to do what I did?

ALEX: I'm not sure.

DEMISSIE: Are you saying that morally you consider yourself superior?

ALEX: No.

DEMISSIE: Alex runs the world everyone! Alex will not sanction torture, Alex will not bite the hand that beats him… So then nothing has happened to him, no one has hurt him. Yet.

ALEX: Are you saying you **want** *them to torture you?*

DEMISSIE: I'm saying you have never made a decision, never stood by a single idea in your whole fucked-up life.

ALEX: Unlike yourself.

DEMISSIE: I can't control what these feelings do to me..In the moment of madness when I plant the bomb, I can't resist my emotions any more than you can resist having to stand and salute the superiors you have grown to despise… (He shakes his head.) And your alliance keep asking me the same question, this… obsession that your enemy must have a name: "Who finances you? Who organises you? Who arms you? And who harbours you?" And there is no one. Many of us here who are guilty, of which I am one, we are a one man band. Thousands, perhaps millions of us, and no one imagines the simplest question: WHY? And the answer is maybe simple. Every morning, I can observe the cellophane wrapping placed around my box of rain, the nice font, the colours, and the very pleasing nature of its design, and wonder if it's really free. A simple thing. This box of rain. Or am I to receive a bill for every box I have drank from, when, and if, the day comes that I am lucky enough to leave Camp Zero?

ALEX hears footsteps approaching.

ALEX: I need to go…

DEMISSIE: Give me a cigarette.

ALEX hands one to DEMISSIE, and goes, as Soldier 1 appears. Soldier 1 stops and regards DEMISSIE's cage. They face each other.

SOLDIER 1: *(To DEMISSIE.)* **You know the drill.**

DEMISSIE steps to the back of the cage, and kneels down, his back turned, his hands behind his back. SOLDIER 1 takes out a syringe and inserts it into DEMISSIE's neck. He collapses. SOLDIER 1 speaks into a walkie-talkie.

Rain Base, I'm at Cage 1136. Detainee disabled. Shall I proceed? Over.

SOLDIER 1 waits. A crackle.

VOICE: **Proceed. Over.**

SOLDIER 1 gets the box of rain and carries it to DEMISSIE's side. The soldier takes DEMISSIE's wrist, slices the vein with a knife, and places DEMISSIE's bleeding wrist on the edge of the box. The SOLDIER steps back.

SOLDIER 1: **Cage 1136, complete. Over.**

SOLDIER 1 pockets the blade and leaves.

DEMISSIE lies where the SOLDIER left him, unconscious, his wrist bleeding into the box of rain.

TWENTY-TWO

The hideout. Night. TOM, still in the middle of packing his bag. His shirt is undone, and he is distracted by the cuts and bruises on his torso.

TOM: **How many days since them presidents isn't it?**

Silence.

Twelve, thirteen?

Silence.

And you're right. I can't forget. End of the rope. And the presidents got happy, isn't it? I don't forget. But I still don't want this. Bick, Pricey, days and nights and jars of beer. I

don't have much but it's waiting for me, you know what I'm saying? And I want to be home isn't it? Don't need nothing else.

ALEX: You can't even read a compass.

TOM: Time to learn isn't it? I go out there, and...

ALEX: And it's just bush. *Miles* off bush. I told you.

TOM: Isn't it? But basically, it's straight on for about six hundred miles, and turn right at the Texaco garage, yeah?

TOM puts his shirt on, gets his bag, his coat, and opens the door.

Good luck. S'cold.

He waits.

ALEX: Just go.

ALEX hugs TOM. A blinding light grows on them. They stare into it

Get away from the door!!

TOM watches the light.

Get away!!!

TOM closes the door, and the light grows stronger, washed in with the approaching roar of a helicopter.

TOM: Too late isn't it?

The helicopter is above them and the wind of its rotors whips through the room.

ALEX: *Fuck...*

ALEX and TOM get down, sheltering from the light and the wind of the rotors. Bullets splatter the wall behind them.

FUCK!!!

They press themselves hard against the floor.

TOM: (Suddenly.) *We'll kill ourselves.*

ALEX: **What?**

TOM: **Ain't being taken alive isn't it?**

ALEX: **Kill ourselves, and they win.**

TOM: **Winning's not everything.**

ALEX: **So how do you want to die?**

TOM: **What?**

ALEX: **If we kill ourselves, how do you want to die?**

Beat.

TOM: **I'll need to give it some more thought isn't it.**

More bullets.

ALEX: **Take as long as you want…**

TWENTY-THREE

The camp. The MAJOR, and ALEX.

MAJOR: *I'm uneasy at this line of questioning, it's not procedure.*

ALEX: *I appreciate that sir.*

MAJOR: *You're a live wire Brines, it's no secret. I want you where I can see you.*

ALEX: *How is Corporal Merson sir, since the demonstration?*

MAJOR: *That's not why you asked to see me.*

ALEX: *No sir.*

MAJOR: *So stick to your question.*

ALEX: *The prisoner in Cage 1136 sir.*

MAJOR: *What about him?*

ALEX: *He's gone.*

MAJOR: *So I understand.*

ALEX: *He was there last night.*

MAJOR: How do you know the man?

ALEX: I was present at several of his interrogation sessions. We spoke about him / some time ago…

MAJOR: I remember.

The MAJOR hands ALEX a file.

According to this report he died as a result of manipulative self injurious behaviour.

ALEX: And is that what's been recorded?

MAJOR: He left a note, if that's what you mean.

ALEX: Who found it?

MAJOR: It'll be on file.

ALEX: (Reading.) 'I committed suicide because of the brutality of my crimes.' When I spoke to him last night, he didn't appear suicidal.

MAJOR: Spoke? No one is to interact with The Others unless / delivering rain, or…

ALEX: No sir. Only since the day I was transferred from Side One, I've found it impossible to sleep. I've taken to wandering the compound at night, watching the cages. Muleneh's section is more empty than I remember at any time since I've been here sir. I asked around…

MAJOR: Asked who?

ALEX: If one needs to know anything that's happening in the Camp it's always best to ask a chef sir.

MAJOR: So I hear.

ALEX: Intensification.

No answer.

And this evening Muleneh's cage is empty.

The MAJOR puts out his hand for the report. SYRAH enters.

MAJOR: If we pursue this any further I can smell trouble for you Lieutenant. If there's nothing else, you should get out of my sight. (To SYRAH.) Alright?

SYRAH smiles.

ALEX: *How did he kill himself sir? It doesn't say.*

MAJOR: *He cut his wrists. Okay, we're done.*

The MAJOR goes to SYRAH.

ALEX: *'Demissie Muluneh died by…' Yes, I saw that, but I asked how he killed himself. All prisoners have their hands bound 24 hours a day. Someone else would have had to cut his wrists.*

Beat.

MAJOR: *(To SYRAH.) Excuse me.*

The MAJOR grabs some more paperwork.

Perhaps you'd like to read this as well.

ALEX: *What is it?*

SYRAH: *(Seamlessly.) A report on you, Lieutenant Brines. All of it filed since you were first before myself and the Major.*

MAJOR: *(To SYRAH.) Nice.*

SYRAH: *Reluctance to translate. Reluctance to prosecute the interrogator's point of view.*

MAJOR: *Constant concerns about you Brines, and now you confess to speaking to the deceased the night before he died, and you question the authenticity of the report into his suicide. What the fuck's going on with you?*

ALEX: *I don't have a name for it sir.*

MAJOR: *A name? It's fucking stupidity! Are you stupid?*

ALEX: *No sir. I'm as shocked as you are. It's not like me to behave in this way… (Of the report.) Do you really intend to file that?*

SYRAH: *He's out of line.*

ALEX: *Where did the blade come from? Where did the prisoner get the pen?*

MAJOR: *Guard!*

ALEX: *THIS IS A CULL.*

MAJOR: *What? A what?*

ALEX: *Demissie Muluneh is the twenty-third prisoner at Camp Zero to commit suicide in a month. How? Why are so many prisoners suddenly killing themselves? Or is this a cull sir?*

Beat.

MAJOR: *I suspect you're finished here Brines.*

ALEX: *You've got no intention of putting these people on trial.*

MAJOR: *You'd need to take that up with / my superiors, like I told you before, we're given our…*

ALEX: *This is what intensification means. 'Ship 'em out, ship 'em in'*

MAJOR: *What?*

ALEX: (Bitter.) *Camp humour, sir.* (To SYRAH.) *It's a phrase.*

The MAJOR stops, regards ALEX.

MAJOR: (Quietly.) *People like you Brines, you get stung by your conscience, the world tumbles in, and suddenly it's all about you, and what you feel. But it's not, is it?*

MAJOR goes to the door.

You are suspended from all duties with immediate effect. All personal possessions will be confiscated, and you will be imprisoned until further notice. Guard!

Helicopters lift off. The MAJOR goes to SYRAH.

SYRAH: (Quieter, to the MAJOR.) *You know it's today. Listen, I'm coming back. I've applied for married quarters. Even when the baby's born, I need to be here.*

MAJOR: *What time do you go?*

SYRAH: (Mock annoyance.) *I told you.*

MAJOR: *I know. Thirteen hundred hours.* (Looks forlornly at his watch.) *An hour.*

Lights.

TWENTY-FOUR

A cell in the camp prison block. ALEX sits against the wall, his hands bound. DEMISSIE stands before him. There is the continued sound of helicopters coming and going, muttered voices, shuffling feet, cages opening and closing.

ALEX listens, far away. Until…

ALEX: …*what?*

DEMISSIE: *Concentrate.*

ALEX: *The helicopters…*

DEMISSIE: *Ship 'em out, ship 'em in.*

ALEX: *What did you ask me?*

DEMISSIE: *I asked, when you sleep in your bed, do you remember me? Do you ask yourself who I really am?*

ALEX: *Of course I do. You're Demissie Muleneh. You're dead.*

DEMISSIE: *You didn't kill me.*

ALEX: *No.*

DEMISSIE: *But you let someone else kill me.*

ALEX: *I went and I spoke about your death.*

DEMISSIE: *You did your bit.*

ALEX: *Yes.*

DEMISSIE: *So do more.*

ALEX: *Go away.*

DEMISSIE: *I'm staying.*

ALEX: *I can't buy explosives.*

DEMISSIE: *I know.*

ALEX: *You planted a bomb, and you killed a man.*

DEMISSIE: *(Agrees.) For me, it's too late. But I also asked you, what do you want?*

ALEX: *I want to be heard.*

DEMISSIE: So speak. There's no excuse.

TOM enters. ALEX stops, looks to where DEMISSIE was. He's gone. TOM is limping, his face bruised.

ALEX: Jesus… Did you see a doctor?

TOM: Doctor. Everyone isn't it? People coming in from the camp to get a look at me… (Nods towards the door.) *Guard says we can have ten minutes… Cosy.*

TOM leans forward suddenly, growling in pain.

ALEX: It's alright… It's okay…

TOM: Fucked isn't it?…

ALEX: Tom.

TOM: I want to die.

ALEX: No you don't. Jesus, I'm in this cell because I can't keep my mouth shut, and now you walk in and you're another example of this place right here before me.

TOM: You got to speak to my mum.

ALEX: Look at you…

TOM: Tell her I was one of the boys for a bit isn't it?

ALEX: Tom…

TOM: I know how to top myself, tried it twice when I was a kid.

ALEX: Every hour, there's people leaving. Prisoners arriving.

TOM: Get me home.

TOM cries still, and ALEX holds him. Waits, until…

ALEX: We've looked out for each other. Yeah?

TOM: Isn't it.

ALEX: They praised you, didn't they? In the recruiting office. They said they needed good men, and they got one, and then they did this to you. This whole camp is about justice, so is this what justice means…?… Torturing them Tom, killing the fuckers…in the last month, twenty-three 'suicides'…

TOM: Isn't it.

*ALEX: Twenty-three fucking suicides, and I'm going to get out of this
cell in ten days and I'm thinking FUCK THIS, they'll put me on
toilet duties till they think I've learnt my lesson, and then I'll be
posted to the most far off shit hole they can imagine…*

TOM: Siberian Sally.

ALEX: What?

*TOM: Sarge tells us they've got a camp up in Russia, watch your step
or you'll end up being a Siberian Sally.*

*ALEX: Yeah? Okay, so that's… I'm… So I've got like…a week,
maybe not that, but I've got time to write it…*

TOM: Write what?

ALEX: A book.

TOM sneers.

*ALEX: It's all I can think of… I've been sitting here, I'm asking
myself…what can I do…?… You can't get information out of a
place like this… But I can write. What're they going to do, tie
me up, gag me, well then I'll write it in my head, I can remember
things, I know six fucking languages for Christ's sake… I'm
sitting in here and they think they can squeeze me, shut me up
because I don't want to think like them…*

TOM: Selling our story yeah?

ALEX: Are we?…

TOM: Dunno.

*ALEX: Maybe you're right, maybe that's what it is… So we find some
greedy bastard…someone greedy enough to take a story like ours
and chuck it out there. Yeah?*

TOM: Do we?

*ALEX: There's a fat fucking wad for you, and there's a big bag of cash
for whoever wants to publish it. Let them start a bidding war for
the rights to 'The Camp'.*

TOM: Shit title.

ALEX: *I need you with me.*

TOM: *How much cash we talking about?*

ALEX: *I don't know, I don't know anything about it, but anything I make is yours alright? I don't want the money, I just want / you and me to…*

TOM: *Can't / write a book.*

ALEX: *We'll break camp, we'll find somewhere safe, and we'll make sure the story's told.*

TOM: *What story?*

ALEX: *In the grip of terror we've become reptiles. Hidden in the shadow of a rock, we bludgeon whatever moves.*

TOM: *What?*

ALEX: *It's the introduction.*

TOM: *The day we arrived, / you told me…*

ALEX: *That's before I understood. Our anger, now… It's power. Tom. It's all that's left to us.*

TOM: *Don't feel like power isn't it, sitting here… See my brains…?*

ALEX: *Tom.*

TOM: *Up my arse.*

ALEX: *Come on… I'll write the book, as soon as it's done, I'll come and get you, we'll break out and I'll get you home.*

TOM: *I don't know…*

ALEX: *I need to know you're with me.*

TOM gets to his feet, turns away.

TWENTY-FIVE

The emerging sound of helicopters starts to grow. It becomes a driving swell of music.

TOM and ALEX hit the deck, crawling through the fence of the camp.

The music swells even greater, and they start to run and run until they fall to the floor, exhausted. Lying there, gasping in air, they hear the sound of dogs growling through the music.

ALEX starts to haul TOM up.

TOM: *Fucked…*

ALEX: *… Come on.*

TOM: *Can't…*

ALEX: *Come on.*

TOM: *Said that last time.*

ALEX: *Few more miles…*

TOM: *Eat first isn't it?*

ALEX: *Later.*

TOM: *Now.*

ALEX grabs the bag with the food.

Give it back.

ALEX: *Just walk.*

TOM jumps onto ALEX, riding his back, reaching for the bag that ALEX shelters around the front of his body.

TOM: *Give me food…!! Need food isn't it!*

ALEX: *Get off.*

TOM: *Can't starve me man.*

ALEX: *I said get off!*

ALEX flips TOM off, so that TOM falls flat onto his back. He groans.

TOM: *Back's fucked.*

ALEX: *Here.*

ALEX offers his hand to TOM, and TOM pulls him down, swiftly reverting power, so that he sits on ALEX's chest. He slaps ALEX's face, twists his nose, and sticks his fingers in his eyes.

TOM: *Torture. Fucking torture, eh? See how you like it. Know all about torture me and you isn't it? (He stretches ALEX's nose.) Torture you now. (He sticks his fingers in ALEX's eyes. ALEX screams.) Make you suffer. Like me... (Slaps him round the face.) See? Back's fucked...legs fucked, and you make me swim, make me run. See? You KNOW what they did to me, and you make me run. See? And now you won't let me eat. (Screams into ALEX's ear.) I AM FUCKING HUNGRY!!! (He slaps him again.) I AM TIRED, AND I CAN'T WALK ANOTHER FUCKING STEP UNTIL I EAT.*

ALEX summons all his strength and flips TOM off. They lie there in silence, weak from hunger. TOM drags a map from his pocket.

Where is it we're going?...

ALEX: *Shore's here...*

He points at the map.

TOM: *Port's there... Other side of the island...*

ALEX: *Exactly.*

They are too tired to move.

Silence.

TOM pulls the package from ALEX's army issue backpack. TOM tests the weight of it.

TOM: *All this trouble isn't it?*

ALEX: *I'll put it back.*

TOM: *Can I read some?*

ALEX: *We'll have to unwrap everything.*

TOM: *Yeah... Tired anyway... Fucked man.*

TOM hands the book over to ALEX, lies back.

Wisden. That's the only book gets near me isn't it? Averages, wickets.

ALEX: Cricket?

TOM: Always wanted to. Trent Bridge when I was a kid isn't it?

ALEX: Do you play?

TOM: No chance, mates don't like it. Footie isn't it? Always footie.

TOM sleeps. ALEX sits in the silence. He lays his head forward, resting his forehead on the bulk of the book.

DEMISSIE appears.

DEMISSIE: Is this the sleep of the just?

DEMISSIE takes the book from ALEX.

ALEX: (Waking.) *Have you come to help me…?*

DEMISSIE feels the book's weight, just like TOM. He hands the book back. SYRAH appears.

SYRAH: Let me feel it.

ALEX hands the book to her.

ALEX: It's heavy.

SYRAH: So?

ALEX: I mean, in your condition, it's heavy.

DEMISSIE: Heavy shit.

SYRAH: Or just shit.

The MAJOR appears.

MAJOR: I hope there's a dedication inside.

ALEX: I can do one.

MAJOR: To our baby.

SYRAH: We're going to call it Demissie.

DEMISSIE: Maybe he hasn't painted you in a very good light.

SYRAH: My conscience is clean.

DEMISSIE: Well then, so must be mine.

MAJOR: Not possible I'm afraid.

SYRAH: *You're one of The Others.*

MAJOR: *Nice.*

ALEX: *Nice.*

The helicopter noise returns. It gets closer, ALEX stares up at it.

MAJOR: *You really should move.*

ALEX: *I can't.*

The noise gets closer and ALEX shrinks towards the ground as the helicopter threatens to crush him. The others leave. ALEX groans as the helicopter noise burns into his brain. TOM wakes.

TOM: *Talking to yourself isn't it?*

Once more, the growing sound again of an approaching helicopter, and distant dogs can be heard. ALEX drags TOM to his feet.

Don't take them long to catch up isn't it?

They head for the path. TOM grabs ALEX's back pack from the ground, and chucks it to him.

Don't forget the book!

ALEX catches the bag and heads off. TOM follows.

(To himself.) Cunt.

TWENTY-SIX

Early early morning.

The hideout. In the distance, the hovering sound of a helicopter. ALEX and TOM lie on the floor. Outside, is the MAJOR, his voice comes to us through a megaphone.

MAJOR: **Zero, zero, five, four, seven, eight, zero, zero, zero, two, four, six, seven, eight, zero, zero, zero, zero, five, zero, two, four, seven, six, zero, zero, four, zero, four, zero, zero,**

zero, zero. (Beat.) You could've rung that one. I know they gave it to you. Or there was the 24 hour line. It's open any time, that's why it's 24 hours. I don't think we're being unreasonable. You're the one who mentioned the book, so what are we supposed to do? Forget about it?

TOM: How did you find us?

ALEX: Don't talk to them.

A round of bullets hits the back wall.

TOM: *Fuck this.*

ALEX: Stay calm.

TOM: I am. I'm trained isn't it?

TOM grabs the package holding the book and runs to the window.

It's here!! You can have it!!! *I'm innocent!! I'm being held against my will!! HELP ME! HELP ME!!!*

ALEX drags TOM down again, there is another round of bullets.

They just want the book you dozy bastard, why can't you understand that?!!

ALEX: *They've been pumping the room with live ammunition for the last half an hour, you think they're going to let us walk away?!!*

TOM: Warnings isn't it? We just need to strike a deal.

MAJOR: The book boys. Do we have to come in and get it, or are you bringing it out?

TOM: *Yeah!! Just give / us a minute, we're on our way…*

ALEX pulls TOM's head close to his own.

ALEX: *Who are these people?*

TOM: You know who they are.

ALEX: *Think.*

MAJOR: Boys?

ALEX: They'll kill us.

TOM: **No.**

ALEX: *Yes. And I don't want us to die for nothing.*

TOM starts to laugh.

TOM: *Us?* It's always us. You're the only 'us' around here isn't it? I'm just… I went to that camp and I came out a corporal. Got the stripes and I'm showing them off. I'm walking out here with my head held high. I made a mistake, but I want to put it behind me, you know what I'm saying?

ALEX: That won't work.

TOM: We give them what they want, we take the rap, and it's done. Works for me.

ALEX: *I promised myself…*

TOM: The longer I keep listening to you, the less chance I've got of *ever* being happy again, you know what I'm saying? And happiness is a big part of my life, it's what I like to be, am I making sense isn't it?

ALEX: This *is* for happiness.

TOM: Your face is happy?

ALEX: That's 'cos you're stressing me out. I've never been on the *verge* of so much happiness.

TOM: Well I'm lying here grovelling over a fucking *BOOK* that's pissing all over my life, and you won't even let me read the fucking thing isn't it?

ALEX: That's what I'm trying to tell you!

TOM: What is?

ALEX: The book's…the book's just…

Another round of bullets. Until…

MAJOR: Boys? Are we staying here all night? Middle of the bush, pissing about over a book. So much going on in the world guys, so many other battles to fight. Do you know how many battles we fight? On your behalf?

ALEX grabs the package.

ALEX: Right.

MAJOR: Battles for continuity. Battles for agreement.

TOM: Halleluah.

MAJOR: A battle to sustain the core of our economic and social infrastructure.

ALEX starts to open the wrapping around the book, (of which there is a lot).

TOM: Get in there.

MAJOR: This is what The Others will bring down. In their clamour. It's not just about killing and maiming. And if that core goes down, then forget publishing books guys. The whole grid collapses, and we return to being cavemen.

TOM: Knew you'd see sense.

TOM starts to help ALEX with the unwrapping.

MAJOR: Skint, into the bargain. It sounds petulant, but it hurts us the way people like yourselves behave. You guys *are* listening aren't you?

TOM and ALEX carry on undoing the wrapping, growing more desperate as the scene continues, and each layer that comes off reveals another layer beneath. It is endless, as futile an activity as the situation they are in. The dialogue that evolves is played one across the other.

Put it this way. If it was your birthday, and the alliance spent a whole afternoon baking a cake and used the type of ingredients it thinks are good for you, and you said you didn't want the cake unless it take this out of it, and that out of it, can you imagine how hurtful that would be? It takes a lot of effort. *Someone* has to be responsible for baking the cake.

TOM: *Fuck's sake.*

ALEX: (Of the wrapping.) Nearly there.

TOM: How much wrapping you put on man?

MAJOR: And you forget, which the alliance reminds us we mustn't, how this world was *one*.

TOM: *Just give it them like it is, isn't it?!*

ALEX: *Wait.*

MAJOR: The world, boys, was *one* at the time of creation.

TOM: *Just take it out to them like it is.*

MAJOR: No one belonged to anyone.

ALEX: Out?

MAJOR: *Nothing* belonged to anyone.

TOM: Let them undo it.

MAJOR: And it never has.

ALEX: Them?

TOM: *Who the fuck else is out there?!!*

ALEX: I don't know what you're talking about.

ALEX resumes the struggle with the wrapping.

MAJOR: No one has the right to tell the alliance to get the fuck off them, or their resources…

TOM: So what you doing?

ALEX: Where's the pen?

MAJOR: Because whoever signed and sealed any of that?

TOM: Alex.

MAJOR: Treaties, international laws.

TOM: *What you doing?*

MAJOR: Set up by who?

The wrapping is undone. There is now just a brown manilla envelope, with a substantial pile of A4 pages inside.

ALEX: I said, where's the pen?

MAJOR: *Who the fuck gave anyone the right to impose any treaties, or laws?*

TOM: **What pen?**

ALEX grabs at their collection of bags and belongings, rooting through them for a pen.

MAJOR: **Where is it signed, in the very first instance, that so and so has the authority to act with that level of authority?**

ALEX: **I just want a pen...** *Can't come all this way and there's no fucking pen...*

MAJOR: **And so let's agree on the Jenga principal.**

ALEX: *Give me the pen.*

MAJOR: **Have you played Jenga? Pull one brick, and everything is nothing.**

TOM: **What pen, I haven't got any fucking pen...**

ALEX: **I know you've got it...**

MAJOR: **We are living in an age of Jenga, where the alliance is utterly within its rights to go out and do what the fuck** *it* **wants.**

ALEX suddenly grabs TOM from behind, surprising him by the power of his assault. He pulls him to the floor, his arms locked around TOM's throat.

ALEX: **I want the pen so I can write, I** *need* **to write. Now. And I want the pen.**

TOM: (Choking, terrified.) **Alex...**

ALEX: **I WANT THE PEN...**

TOM: **Wh...**

ALEX: **I WANT THE PEN...**

TOM: **...**

ALEX: **This can go on for hours, it's been known to go on for weeks.**

TOM can barely breathe and ALEX keeps squeezing.

I want the pen, because right now I need to write.

TOM is dying.

Tell me where it is.

MAJOR: I've been given an option.

ALEX's trance is broken by the interruption of the MAJOR, and he stops, TOM is able to roll free, coughing, choking, vomiting.

TOM: *Fucking nutter…you nearly fucking, you nearly fucking…!!!*

ALEX: I wanted the pen… *You don't understand… I haven't written the book… I couldn't write it…and so I need a pen… I need to write it…*

TOM: *Fuck.*

TOM drags himself to his feet, goes to the door and opens it. The sound of a single shot. TOM falls back, dead. ALEX goes to him.

MAJOR: (Screaming into the megaphone.) *Who's firing!! … Who told any of you to fire!!!!*

Silence.

Is he alive?

ALEX kneels beside TOM, he is weeping.

It might sound a little callous, bearing in mind your friend's sudden death, but the option, which I received by text just a second ago, was that I didn't have to kill the both of you, not right away. I can take one of you back to the camp. Alive. I suppose half the problem's solved for us, so thanks for that.

It's only a book, barely significant in the scheme of things, but you know the alliance has to stop you.

Whilst we're being sincere, I should say, Lieutenant Brines, that I haven't been entirely honest. Your idea for the book was common knowledge to me from its conception, and you were under observation the second you were released from your cell. Because of that, it feels appropriate to offer you some dignity and allow your torture, because you know that before we kill you, we *will* have to torture you, to be dispensed with out here in the wilderness, where no one can witness your indignity. (Beat.) Lieutenant?

ALEX has taken the mobile phone from TOM's back pack. He dials, pulling out the pages of A4 paper from inside the manilla envelope, as he waits for the phone to answer. We can see that they are blank on both sides, that the book is unwritten, and as he talks on the mobile, he slowly covers TOM's body, head to toe, until there are none left.

ALEX: (Phone.) Baby...? It's me...

MAJOR: Lieutenant?

ALEX: The book's called Zero...

MAJOR: Alex?

ALEX: You'll have to write it down, I'll have to dictate it to you... Make sure the title's right. *Zero*. Nothing else. I was going to call it The Camp, but Tom said it was a shit title...

MAJOR: Do you want five minutes to prepare yourself?

ALEX: Have you got a pen?... Fi... Listen, have you got a pen? I'd write it myself, now, but they're waiting. If you get a pen, I can tell you the first few words and then you need to imagine the rest... How can you?... how can... Who can imagine anything like this...?

MAJOR: Do you want to open the door, or shall we come in?

ALEX: I tried to write it...you *know* they do this, people *know* they do this...but *what* they do...

MAJOR: So much consideration

ALEX: ...and I... *Watching*...like a sickness, dark...soul... Fi...my... How can I *write* that...so many words...to find. I...

MAJOR: You'll be tired.

ALEX: There isn't a book, I...

He stands looking at TOM who is now covered head to foot with the blank paper.

MAJOR: You'll be hungry.

ALEX gets his breath.

ALEX: They're outside. Even if you write down what I tell you and you get the world to read the book, I don't think they'll be bothered. They're not frightened of the truth. What hope have we got? But dry your eyes. I'll dry mine. Come on.

MAJOR: Alex?

ALEX: It has to be written.

MAJOR: Alex.

ALEX: This time.

MAJOR: Right.

ALEX: They're coming. I love you...write down everything I told you about the camp...write it down because now it belongs to you... The first line...write it...finish the book...

The door opens and the MAJOR stands in its frame. He carries a box of rain. He and ALEX stare at each other.

'This is all I can do...this is what I *have* to do. Because this has been my story.'

Lights.